# Contents

| | | |
|---|---|---|
| 1 | What can a PC do? | *1* |
| 2 | Getting deeper into soundcards | *5* |
| 3 | MIDI sequencing | *16* |
| 4 | Hard-disk recording | *23* |
| 5 | Sample/wave editing | *33* |
| 6 | Plug-ins | *35* |
| 7 | Notation and score writing | *38* |
| 8 | Software synthesis | *41* |
| 9 | Internet music | *48* |
| 10 | Intermission | *55* |
| 11 | Tackling Windows | *57* |
| 12 | PC music setups | *66* |
| 13 | The dance music appendium | *74* |
| 14 | The guitarist's appendium | *80* |
| 15 | Frequently asked questions | *84* |
| 16 | Glossary | *95* |
| 17 | Products | *99* |
| 18 | General MIDI | *108* |
| 19 | Contacts | *112* |
| | Index | *114* |

# Acknowledgements

I'd like to express my thanks to anyone who showed even the slightest interest in this project particularly:
Graham for being the perfect test case;
Matt for his comments and untaken advice;
Simon for just being smiley;
Sam for saying 'hey, why don't you write a book';
Seb for his interest and comments on layout;
Katherine for her encouragement and for going to the other side of the world so that she wouldn't be such a distraction;
Brian O'Connell for looking after my interests;
Everyone at 24 Hainthorpe Road for not making too many snide comments about sitting in front of a PC all the time and not coming out for beers;
All the staff and customers of Turnkey whose constant questioning forced me into knowing about all this stuff;
Phil for agreeing to publish it.

The only sources used in the writing of this book were the internet, some old college notes, and what was knocking around in my head.

# Introduction

**C**omputers and music have been used together for years. Back in the 1980's my humble Commodore 64 was a drum machine, an eight track MIDI sequencer and a sampler (a whole 1.6 seconds worth). I even used it at a gig, although it took three minutes to load each song.

Today, the stuff you can do with a PC is staggering, and yet it seems to be a well kept secret. How can a PC be used for music? What software and hardware do I need? Can I produce professional music or is a PC just for mucking about? How does it all connect together with the gear I have already? These are just some of the questions I aim to answer and hopefully these pages will give you an idea of what's possible and suggest a solution to your musical demands.

I've based everything in relation to an IBM compatible PC running Windows 95/98 simply because at this time it's the most popular platform and has the most varied hardware and software available for it. All the concepts in this book are completely applicable to whichever platform you use (except the bit on Windows of course).

It's not my intention to recommend or plug any particular products. The screen shots I have used are there as examples, besides as soon as a screen shot is taken it becomes out of date. Any software you buy may look a little different, but these illustrations are useful, not to mention pretty.

I have tried to be, on the most part, objective, although at times my opinions and experience do burst through. I am always asked for my opinion on what's best and what's possible so it's only fitting that it comes through in the book. Please feel free to disagree with my ranting at any point, I won't be offended.

# What can a PC do?

There are four main areas in which a PC can contribute to music:
- MIDI sequencing
- Hard disk digital audio recording
- Sample/digital audio editing
- Notation

Each is a separate function which can be used completely independently but more often they are combined in a single package.

But which of these do you need? The first question to ask is 'What do I want to do?'. Okay, possible scenarios:

1  I'm a concert pianist and composer. I want to be able to write and print out the score of my latest concerto for a sixty-four piece orchestra.
2  I've got a couple of keyboards and I want to record what I play and then muck about with it.
3  I'm a guitarist in a three piece skiffle band and we want to produce a decent demo.
4  I'm a songwriter and I want to produce an album of my stuff.
5  I'm at art school and I want to produce a sound effects soundtrack to accompany my anarchist plasticine animations.
6  I've got a computer, I might have a sound card, I can't read music but I fancy a go at making some music.

The solutions are:

> 1  Get a professional notation package. Anyone who is used to and comfortable with written music should consider this option.
> 2  Get a MIDI sequencer. If you want to work with electronic instruments, whether you're a Techno head or Vangelis, then you want one of these.
> 3  Get a hard disk recording package and a decent microphone. If you're dealing with 'real' instruments, acoustic guitar, voice etc. then go for this option.
> 4  Get a MIDI sequencing/hard disk recording package. For anyone wanting to use a bit of everything.
> 5  Get a Wave editing package. Applies to people producing lecture tapes, videos, mastering songs and stuff.
> 6  Get some talent. No, most people fall into this category, it's nothing to be ashamed of. Hopefully after reading this tome you'll have a better idea of what you want to do or at least what you should spend your money on.

## But what does it all mean?

### MIDI

This is an acronym (it stands for Musical Instrument Digital Interface) and has nothing to do with the size of your hi-fi.  MIDI was established in the late seventies by major electronic instrument manufacturers as a standard to allow instruments (initially keyboard synthesisers) of different makes to talk to each other.

The sort of messages sent over MIDI are Note On, Note Off, Velocity (how hard the note was struck), Patch Change, in fact almost anything that you can do to a keyboard can be sent over MIDI. In reality this means that you can control the sounds of one keyboard by playing another, but the most important aspect was that the information could be recorded into and played back from a MIDI sequencer.

A MIDI 'device' (synthesiser, sound module, etc.) is usually clever enough to do more than one thing at a time. This is called 'multi-timbrality' the standard being 16 parts. A standard MIDI device can send and receive MIDI information on 16 separate channels, typically one channel for each part. In real terms, this means that you can usually get a MIDI device to play 16 different instruments, independently, at the same time. That's handy.

### MIDI sequencer

This is mostly how a computer has been used in music up to now. The most popular platform has been the Atari ST running

Steinberg's Cubase, then came the Apple Mac, and now the PC is taking over. A MIDI sequencer comes as a software package and they are all pretty similar in what they do. They allow you to record, edit and play back MIDI information, and then usually let you print out the score of your finished masterpiece. Since this is just data, you can muck about with it as much as you like. You can change it around, move it to another note, another channel, another instrument, a different bar, cut, copy and paste it wherever you desire. A simple example would be as follows:

Click on Record, play on your keyboard for a bit, click on Stop and play it back. Oops, hit a wrong note, go into edit and move it to the right pitch. The first two bars were rubbish so delete them. The next bar was inspired so I'll copy and paste that a hundred times. The rest I'll paste onto another track, give it another channel (which makes it sound like another instrument) and play them back together. Pop stardom beckons.

## Hard disk digital audio recording

Everyone with a sound card should be fairly comfortable with the concept of Wave files (*.wav) on a PC. When you start up Windows you are greeted with a kind of hello noise which is a wave file being played back off your hard drive. This is a simple form of hard disk recording. Plug a microphone into your sound card, open Windows Sound Recorder and you can record sound directly onto your hard drive. Nothing new there. It's what you can do with it when it's on your hard drive which makes it interesting.

### Simple example time

Mic up your guitar amp, click on Record, and play like Hendrix with his hair on fire for a few minutes, or strum a few chords if you like. Play it back and grimace at your own ineptitude. Wrong note in the solo, isolate it and use the pitch shift tool to nudge it up a semitone. First chorus was pants, delete it. Second chorus was god like, copy and paste it where the first one should have been and four times at the end for good measure and once in reverse in the middle. Paste a verse onto another track, pitch shift it up a fifth for an instant harmony. Mix down to tape, send it to Sony, sell your soul to the devil, and you're a rock god.

### Sample/wave digital audio editing

A different angle on hard disk recording using a single stereo track recorded onto the hard disk. Take a short piece of audio and muck about with it. Loop it, fade it in and out, crossfade it into another sample, chop it up and change it around. Record a spoken sentence and cut and paste it to say something else. Add effects and dump it into a sampler. Before you know it you're wearing a tie and working for the BBC.

**INFO**

*A* dedicated hard disk recording package can arguably replace a whole studio. You can record multiple tracks, add effects, mixdown and even burn it directly onto a CD. Beats booking studio time.

## Notation

This software allows you to place black dots onto a load of parallel lines. An ability to read music is a definite advantage. Plug a piano into your PC and gasp as the notes appear on the screen as you play. Move the notes around on the screen, delete bum ones, add new ones, change key, change time signature, record multiple parts, and print it all out. Pop down the Albert Hall and wave your arms around in a 'Last night of the Proms' style.

The following chapters cover these four areas in greater depth. First I'd like to try to clarify something. 'Package' is used as a general term to describe a complete solution. So a hard disk digital audio recording package has all you need to record digital audio. Usually this is just software, but can often be associated with a piece of hardware, like a soundcard, as well. There are many interchangeable terms associated with computers and computer music and I will try to highlight them as we go.

# Getting deeper into soundcards

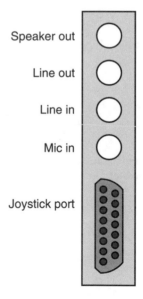

Speaker out

Line out

Line in

Mic in

Joystick port

Figure 2.1 Do you have soundcard already? Have a look for something like this at the back of your computer

efore launching into the four main areas there are a couple of concepts that are very important to grasp, *MIDI* and *audio,* what they are, how they differ and how they relate to each other. Understanding these two facets of computer music will make everything (well, everything to do with computer music) far clearer and easier to cope with.

I've found that the best way to get these concepts across is in relation to the soundcard. What's a soundcard? Well the majority of computers come with the ability to generate sound. Noises that are heard when you open windows, sound effects and music in games and multimedia programs. All these sounds are generated by the soundcard, it's a piece of hardware and it contains an element of both MIDI and audio. All the software described in the following chapters utilises either one or both of these facilities. I'll assume, for the purposes of this chapter, that you do have a soundcard in your PC. If you don't then hopefully this chapter will show you why you should.

The easiest way to find your soundcard is to look at the back of your PC and see if you can spot something resembling Figure 2.1 (there are many different makes of soundcard so it may not look exactly the same as the diagram, but it will be something similar).

In order to hear anything your soundcard may want to produce you need to connect it up. The arrangement of the ins and outs of the soundcard may vary from the diagram. See your soundcard's documentation to check which sockets are which or, alternatively, try plugging things into sockets in a 'trial and error' kind of way.

**Speaker out**
Amplified sound comes out of here. Connect this to unpowered speakers or headphones.

**Line out**
Non-amplified sound comes out of here. This can be connected to an amplifier or your hi-fi or powered speakers.

**Line in**
This is a recording port for anything at line level like a tape player or a mixer.

**Mic in**
This is a recording port for a microphone. You can plug a mic straight in and record any sound you like.

**Joystick port**
You can plug a joystick into here to play games with. This port can also become a MIDI in/out interface with the addition of an adapter cable. This is very handy for us and we'll come back to this later.

A soundcard contains all the necessary hardware to make music on a PC, although at a fairly rudimentary level. In understanding the component parts of the humble soundcard it is possible to grasp the meaning of, and the reason for, all the other bits of hardware that can be used in music making on a PC.

There are two distinct parts to a soundcard and should never be confused with each other: *Audio and MIDI.* It is very important that you understand what each part does and that they are completely different animals.

Figure 2.2 is a simplified representation of a soundcard's components.

Figure 2.2 Soundcard gubbins

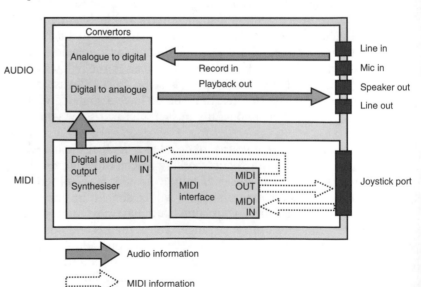

Now, let's look at the two halves of the soundcard in greater depth.

# Audio

Audio is sound, stuff we can hear, sound waves in air, anything you can detect with your ears. Audio can be recorded by converting those sound waves into electrical charges, this is what a microphone does, and that information can be stored onto something, like tape or even a hard-disk.

The audio side of a soundcard allows you to record and play back sound in the same way that you would record onto a tape machine. Plug in a microphone and record your voice, plug in a line level source, like a CD player, and record that and then play it back. Simple really.

What the soundcard is actually doing can be a bit complicated so I'll try to explain it. If it all gets a bit heavy for you then skip the techy bit that follows because this isn't essential information but it really might help you to understand pretty much everything.

## Techy bit

The soundcard contains two integrated circuits, or chips if you like. One converts the incoming electrical or *analogue* signal from the mic etc. into *digital* information which can be understood and stored by the PC. This is called an analogue-to-digital converter (ADC). The other circuit does the complete opposite. It converts the digital information generated by the PC playing back the digital audio, back into an analogue signal that loudspeakers understand and therefore reproduces the sound. This is called a digital-to-analogue converter (DAC). So, digital audio is simply audio which has been through an ADC and is now 'digitised'. The quality of the converters has a direct effect on the sound quality of what you're recording in the same way that something recorded on a cheap and nasty tape recorder won't sound as good as something recorded on an expensive flashy tape machine. The converters on most soundcards are of the cheap and nasty variety, but hey, you have to start somewhere.

The process of A-to-D conversion is called sampling. Now, this term is often misunderstood because of its association with samplers. A sampler does the same thing as a soundcard, in that it digitally records audio but it stores it in RAM (random access memory) and triggers the sound for playback via MIDI. It uses the recorded audio as a MIDI instrument in the same way as playing a piano sound on a synth. A PC samples audio and records it onto the hard-disk where it can be played back like a tape machine. It's a small difference but an essential one. To act like a sampler a PC needs additional hardware in a sampler card which contains its own RAM. Some soundcards do already have this ability, but it's often very limited, in quality and features, compared to an external, professional sampler. Of course, as we speak, software samplers are being developed which will use system RAM or the hard disk to enable a PC to act as a sampler. Even so, it would still trigger the samples as a MIDI device.

Anyway, what sampling does is to look at (sample) the analogue signal several times a second and calculates a single value to represent the signal at each of those times. So, there are two factors involved in sampling which also govern the quality; *sampling rate* and *resolution*.

Sampling rate is measured in hertz (Hz) and denotes the number of times per second that the analogue signal is looked at (or sampled). Resolution or bit rate is the amount of values available to represent that signal, and is measured in bits. This is most easily explained in Figure 2.3.

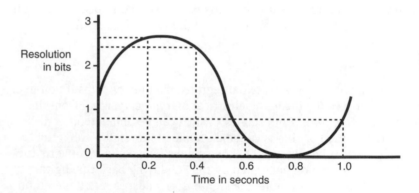

Figure 2.3 Audio signal of 1 second duration sampled at a rate of 5 Hz (five times per second)

Er... no it isn't, let me expand:

**Binary**

Bit = possible values
1 $(2^1)$ = 2
2 $(2^2)$ = 4
4 $(2^4)$ = 16
8 $(2^8)$ = 256
16 $(2^{16})$ = 65536

The curve is an audio signal of one second in length. The sample rate is 5Hz because a measurement is being taken five times during one second. The resolution is 2 bit. The bit is a binary format so one bit would be 2 to the power of 1, two bit would be 2 to the power of 2, three bit 2 to the power of 3 and so on. So 2 bit, or two squared, gives the possibility of 4 (0 to 3) values. Computers can only deal with whole values represented by the 1's and 0's of binary.

So, at 0.2 seconds the signal is measured and is given a value of 3 because that is the nearest whole value. At 0.4 seconds the signal is given a value of 2, at 0.6 – 0, at 0.8 – 0, and 1.0 – 1. The result shown in Figure 2.4 is the computer's representation of that audio signal.

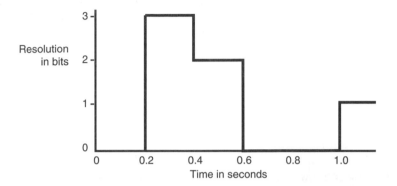

Figure 2.4 The computer's representation of the audio signal sampled at 5 Hz

Close but no cigar. Well the conversion was pretty rubbish and on playback it would sound a lot like noise rather than the nice sine wave that went in. This is because the sample rate and resolution were pitifully low and only useful as an aid to understanding the concept.

The accepted standard of resolution and sample rate is 16 bit at 44.1kHz. That's a bit rate of 65536 (2 to the power of 16) possible values measured at 44100 times a second. This is also known as CD quality because it's the sample quality at which CDs are recorded. So that's a tad more accurate than my example, so accurate in fact that the ear has trouble telling the difference between the recorded version and the real thing.

End of techy bit!

## Soundcards and numbers

The numbers associated with soundcards are often misleading (unintentionally of course). The classic example is with Creative Labs Sound Blaster range. When Creative launched the SB16 many years ago the '16' refered to the fact that it was their first 16 bit soundcard. Their next card was named the AWE32. Now, the '32' no longer refers to bits but to polyphony (or voices), it's still a 16 bit card but the on-board synth can produce 32 voices simultaneously. Similarly with the AWE64, still 16 bit but with 64 note polyphony. Other soundcard manufacturers use the same numbers for the very same reason.

So if that's the case why do we have audio systems which report to be 18, 20 or even 24 bit? Well, the problem is to do with error correction. This is the amount the actual value was moved to reach a whole value. Each time you process a piece of audio on the computer it is subject to further calculations using values which have already been rounded to the nearest whole number. The amount of error correction is, therefore, compounded and there comes a point at which this becomes noticeable in the deterioration of the sound. Upping the bit rate improves this dramatically. The other reason is that people claim that it sounds better – which it probably does but I can't really say that my ears have noticed it, but then my ears have spent far too much time listening to far too loud music.

The other main quality factor involved in the soundcard's ADC and DAC is the level of noise introduced to the signal. This is often referred to as the signal-to-noise ratio. Cheap soundcards with cheap converters create noise. There can be noise inherent in the circuitry and noise picked up by the card from the inside of the PC. Listen to your soundcard playing back an audio file and you'll probably hear a load of hiss as well. A card with a high signal-to-noise ratio can lower the noise interference, when recording, to almost nothing at all.

**INFO**

If a sound is recorded at a low resolution, it will play back at the same quality regardless of which soundcard you put it through.

## Digital ins and outs

One way to bypass all this mucking about with the soundcard's analogue to digital conversion is to get hold of a soundcard with a digital input and output. Now, this is an interface which allows you to record audio onto your PC which is already in the digital domain.

What does all that mean? Let me explain. Digital information (could be digital audio, could be software, could be just a file) can be moved between different digital devices and arrive in the new device exactly in exactly the same state as when it left. Consider a floppy disk. You can copy a file onto a floppy and put it into another PC and the file is exactly the same. That's because it's digital and it's remained in the digital domain throughout the transfer process. Okay, you've got a song recorded as digital audio on your PC. To record (or master) that song onto a tape it has to be converted to analogue again through your soundcard. Now if you were to record the song onto a digital recorder, like DAT (digital audio tape) or a CD writer, you could transfer the song digitally without having to convert back to analogue. This way the DAT receives an exact copy of the original. This is done by connecting the digital out of the soundcard to the digital in of the DAT machine. A DAT machine will generally have far better quality DAC's and ADC's than a soundcard and so playback (and recording) will be of a higher quality.

Now, there's an important point to grasp here. An external device like a DAT machine can have much better quality converters, so, why not use the DAT machine as the audio side of the soundcard and route the recorded digital audio into the PC via the digital input. The conversion is done outside the PC so no internal PC noise is added. Replace the DAT machine with a digital mixing desk and suddenly you have high quality professional inputs, converters and mixing going directly into your PC. Blimey, from a simple soundcard to the potential of professional studio recording in a few simple steps!

So, out of all that all you really need to know is that a soundcard is a piece of hardware that has the ability to digitally record and playback audio. Super.

# MIDI

Your soundcard will contain at least one synthesiser. A synthesiser literally synthesises sounds or instruments. It contains clever circuitry which will produce a sound in response to a MIDI signal. You could see it as an electronic keyboard, tone generator or sound module, which is exactly what it is, but without the box and black and white keys attached. A wavetable soundcard usually contains 128 synthesised sounds which can be played via MIDI. These sounds are laughingly given names like 'piano' and 'violin' and nowadays aren't bad attempts at sounding like the instrument of its name. Instrument sounds are also called 'patches' which is a throwback reference to old analogue synths where sounds were created by joining or patching oscillators and modulators together with cables or patch leads. They can also be called 'programs' for no suitably explored reason.

**WAVETABLE**

*A* form of synthesis that uses actual samples as the basis of sound creation.

Let's get clear on what a MIDI device is. Anything that responds or reacts to MIDI information could be called a MIDI device. Usually this is an electronic musical instrument like a keyboard or synthesiser. MIDI devices without keyboards are often called 'sound modules' or 'tone generators'. The synthesiser on your soundcard is a MIDI device, so is a software synthesiser, a hardware sampler, a MIDI controlled mixer or effects unit. MIDI has become widely used as a control language in all sorts of areas.

MIDI is like hearing a piece of music, but rather than recording it with a microphone you instead write out the score (you have perfect pitch obviously). You could alter the score and give it to a guitarist to play, or to a trombone player, or any other musician who understands notation and you can hear the music played on any other instrument.

So, you haven't recorded the sound, you've recorded a set of instructions which tells a musician how to play that piece of music. You could see the score as MIDI information and the musicians as MIDI devices and maybe this all makes sense.

MIDI is a stream of instructions sent from one MIDI device to another in order to produce a response. The sort of instructions

include 'note on' which contains information telling a MIDI device
to play a note of a certain pitch at a certain velocity or loudness.
'pitch bend' which tells the device to apply a bend in pitch to the
sound currently being made. 'program change' which tells the
device to choose another instrument. There are 128 different
instructions or 'controllers' available in MIDI and can be applied to
all sorts of stuff. They could control the faders on a MIDI mixing
desk, the depth of effect on a MIDI controlled effects unit, or even
the movement of lights on a MIDI controlled lighting rig.

Keeping it simple you could use a piece of software into which
you place a sequence of notes (let's call it a sequencer), your PC
then sends that information as MIDI to your soundcard's synth. The
synth then happily plays these notes back to you with the
instrument sound of your choosing.

Even easier would be to plug a music keyboard into the PC so
that you could just play the keys and let the computer record what
you are playing. The computer is recording MIDI information – it is
logging what notes you played at what time and sending this
information to your soundcard's synth, which then does what it's
told. No actual sound is being recorded here, just instructions.

## Connecting MIDI devices to your PC

How do we connect other MIDI devices, like a keyboard, to the
computer? We need that essential bit of gear called the MIDI
interface. A PC can become a true MIDI device by installing a MIDI
interface so it has the ability to send and receive MIDI information
outside of itself. Every MIDI device has an interface consisting of at
least one, 5 pin circular socket, or 5 pin 'DIN'. A DIN used to be an
audio connection and was very popular when MIDI was invented, so
it was chosen as a good format. The pin connections inside the
cables and sockets differ from the audio type so you must get MIDI
cables and not old audio DIN cables to connect MIDI stuff together.
Anyway, most MIDI devices have two sockets, one labelled MIDI IN
to receive information, one labelled MIDI OUT to send. Some have a
third labelled MIDI THRU, this routes whatever information is
coming into the IN straight back out allowing you to chain several
MIDI devices together.

The simplest of MIDI interfaces is one incorporated into your
soundcard. The joystick port can be configured to act as a MIDI
interface. Those clever bods at Roland came up with a driver called
the MPU-401 (catchy name), which is included with Windows, to
make this happen. All you need is a special adapter cable and you
have one MIDI IN and OUT. Interfaces can provide more than one
MIDI port. A MIDI port can send and receive MIDI over 16 MIDI
channels. A MIDI device with one MIDI port can respond on 16 MIDI
channels. By having more ports you can send 16 channels to
separate MIDI devices independently. Ideally you should have a port

for each MIDI device. Interfaces with 8 MIDI ports are common. This gives a total of 128 separate MIDI channels, so you could have 128 instrument sounds being played from your sequencer, more than enough for most people. MIDI interfaces are either computer cards fitted internally with a bunch of cables hanging off the back, or an external unit connecting through the serial or parallel port. All the MIDI ports are accessed through the software sequencer described in the next chapter.

To connect it up all you would need is a MIDI cable between your keyboard's MIDI OUT port to the computer's MIDI IN (provided by an interface). The computer could then receive all the information generated by playing the keyboard and trigger the sounds off your soundcard, or record the information into a sequencer. Alternatively you could route that MIDI information out to an external MIDI device by connecting the MIDI OUT of the computer to the MIDI IN of the external MIDI device. So, instead of using the rubbish sounds generated by your soundcard's synth, you can plug your MIDI performance into a very expensive synthesiser or sampler and feel astonished at how good you sound.

A good point to make here is that the actual sound comes out of whatever MIDI device you plug your MIDI information into. If you are using your soundcard's synth then the sound will come out of the soundcard's output, along with any audio. If you are using an external MIDI device then the sound will come out of that device. Seems obvious but you have no idea how many people miss this completely. If you want to know what this looks like then check out Chapter 12 'PC Music Setups' on page 66.

But why don't you just record the keyboard live? Well, because MIDI can be manipulated and edited and programmed to do all sorts of things and can be recorded without the need to be able to play an instrument, and can sound like a whole orchestra without having to hire one. I'll go into the joys of MIDI sequencing in the next chapter, but a simple example would be that you play in a few bars of a song on a keyboard but you're a bit of a sloppy player so your timing is awful and you've played a couple of bum notes. As MIDI is just simple data you can tell the computer to put all the notes you played on an even beat, then simply delete the notes which were wrong. You initially played the song with a piano sound but now you think it would sound better as a trumpet, no problem, tell the computer to change the sound that's being used. This would be impossible to do if the performance was recorded live as audio.

I hope that you have fully grasped the two concepts of MIDI and audio, as they can lead in very different musical directions, affect your choices of software and hardware and allow you to show off to your friends because you know what you're talking about.

If you look back a few pages at the soundcard diagram (Figure 2.2) you should be able to recognise the two distinct MIDI and audio parts.

## SUMMARY

So, to summarise. Your soundcard has two functions. It can record and play back real sound like a tape deck, and it can send and receive MIDI information which it can route through its onboard synthesiser to sound like a poor representation of a whole orchestra.

Now then, you can buy bits of hardware which will specialise in the audio *or* the MIDI bit and are of a much higher standard than your all-in-one jobby.

For instance: Emagic's Audiowerk8 is an 18bit, 2in/8out audio recording card. Its not a soundcard because it has no synth on board or MIDI capabilities. It simply records sound in stereo and can play it back through a choice of 8 outputs allowing you to separate audio tracks out of a PC through a mixing desk. It's an audio card.

Midiman's Winman 4x4 is a MIDI interface with four separate MIDI ports allowing four MIDI devices to be attached to the PC completely independently. It has no ability to record audio and has no synth on board. It acts as a MIDI connection to external synthesisers and sound modules like a Roland JV1080, Yamaha MU90, Korg Trinity, or any other MIDI device. It's simply a MIDI interface and routes MIDI information in and out of the PC.

## General MIDI (GM)

Although MIDI is a standard, 16 channels, 128 values etc. there was originally no correlation between MIDI devices from different manufacturers, or between devices from the same manufacturer for that matter. If you created a piece of music using one MIDI device and then played it back through a different one, the instruments you chose may not be the same on both devices. For instance, instrument number 1 on the original device may be a piano sound, on the second device it may be a sitar. That's a bit annoying. So you've created a masterpiece MIDI sequence using your soundcard's synth and now you've taken the MIDI file to a proper studio to play the sequence through a posh and expensive sound module. Unfortunately all the sounds are wrong and it sounds terrible, and one particular sound you used they don't even have. You then have to spend hours finding out where the right patches are and programming something to sound like the sound you wanted.

Luckily the powers that be recognised this problem and got their heads together to produce a solution, and they did, and they called it General MIDI.

General MIDI denotes that any supporting MIDI device will contain a minimum of 128 defined instrument sounds (for a full list see the 'General MIDI Instrument List' on page 108) beginning with Piano as the first patch, then going through keyboard instruments, strings, brass, basses, guitars, wind, synth sounds, pads, percussion, sound effects ending up with sound 128 as a gunshot (why they thought that a gunshot was a vital sound is anyone's guess). There would also be half a dozen drum kits covering rock, jazz, analogue and orchestral. The drum kits would always respond on channel 10 and the individual drum sounds are mapped to specified key numbers (see page 110).

### MIDI file

*A* MIDI sequence, as described in the next chapter, can be saved as a MIDI file which can be read by any other sequencer or MIDI file player.

### INFO

*T*he terms 'patch', 'GM sound' 'GM voice' are used pretty well interchangeably in MIDI sequencing circles.

The majority of soundcards conform roughly to General MIDI. So, now that you've created your fantastic MIDI file you can take it down a studio and plug it into a posh device which has a General MIDI sticker on it and all the sounds will be correct, but probably of a much more realistic quality. Fantastic. This means you can share MIDI files with other people and when they play them back through their own soundcard or GM device the music will sound more or less as you intended it.

Loads of MIDI devices conform to GM nowadays. Most have far more than the standard 128. Roland and Yamaha have come up with their own, expanded versions of GM. Roland's GS standard offers around 250 sounds, small variations on the 128 and adds control for reverb and chorus effects. Yamaha's XG standard goes further to produce over 700 sounds, again variations on the 128, a few more drum kits and lots of controls for all kinds of interesting effects. Essentially they offer GM compatibility, but if you are using equipment with GS or XG functions then you can have much more control over the sounds.

As the GM patches are defined they are often referred to by their given names, rather than by patch number. So, rather than selecting patch number 1 for piano, you could simply select 'piano'. Most software sequencers allow you to select a GM sound by name which makes the whole thing a lot more friendly, which is nice.

Figure 2.5 Logos for General MIDI, Roland's GS, and Yamaha's XG standards

There's more on General MIDI in Chapter 18.

# 3 ★ MIDI sequencing

**M**any years ago in the heady days of analogue synthesis, when people mucked about with voltage controlled oscillators, amplifiers and filters all strung together with a tangle of patch leads, some bright spark came up with the idea of applying a cyclic timing device to the voltage input. Voltage level controlled the frequency of the oscillators and, therefore, pitch, so by varying the voltage you could play different notes. With this new timing device you could set different voltages (and therefore pitch) and get the timer to trigger them in 'sequence'. These devices or 'sequencers' usually consisted of eight parts and can be heard all over early 1980's pop music. Depeche Mode, Yazoo, Human League, Gary Numan along with Kraftwerk, Vangelis and Jean-Michel Jarre are good examples, or not, depending on your taste.

As synthesisers went digital, control voltage gave way to MIDI, and analogue circuitry and potentiometers gave way to data and memory. Although the implementation of recording and playing back MIDI data far outstripped the capabilities of the old analogue sequencers, the name stuck, and the increasingly inaccurate 'sequencer' remains.

The possibilities now available in a software MIDI sequencing package are far beyond simply stringing a sequence of notes together. It's become a full on programming language and can be used to manipulate an increasingly varied array of products and functions. In this chapter I hope to shed a little light on the simpler functions of a MIDI sequencer so that you'll get an idea of what you could do with one.

The basic concept of the modern MIDI sequencer is the ability to record, edit and play back MIDI data. Software sequencers, of which there are several brands, generally follow the same format and have very similar editing possibilities. So the following examples should be applicable to whatever sequencer you are using.

## The arrange window

Also known as the track window, the arrange window displays an overview of what has been recorded. It consists of a vertical list of tracks and a timebase display showing blocks of data that have been recorded relative to time. The time base is usually shown in bars and beats but this can also be real time in seconds. This is far easier to show rather than to describe (Figure 3.1).

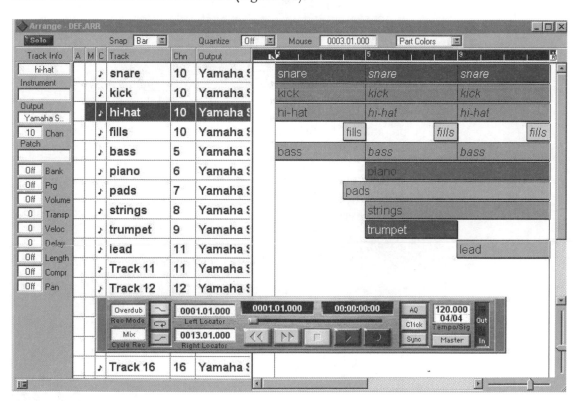

Figure 3.1 The arrange window in Steinberg's Cubase VST

On the left hand side you can see a list of MIDI tracks. Each track has been given a name and there's also information on allocated MIDI channel and what MIDI device the track is set to for output. In this case it's a Yamaha MIDI device. Each track is playing a different instrument so each track has to be on a separate MIDI channel, with the exception of the four drum tracks at the top.

The drum kits on the Yamaha device are accessed on channel 10 so all four drum tracks will be on this channel. I have used different tracks to record the drums as I find it easier to edit each part

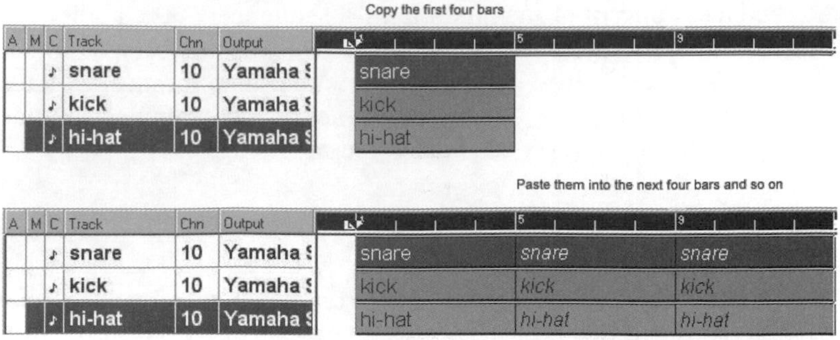

Figure 3.2 Copy and paste – one of the wonders of the software sequencing

Copy the first four bars

| A | M | C | Track | Chn | Output | | 5 | | 9 | |
|---|---|---|-------|-----|--------|---|---|---|---|---|
| | | ♪ | snare | 10 | Yamaha S | snare | | | | |
| | | ♪ | kick | 10 | Yamaha S | kick | | | | |
| | | ♪ | hi-hat | 10 | Yamaha S | hi-hat | | | | |

Paste them into the next four bars and so on

| A | M | C | Track | Chn | Output | | 5 | | 9 | |
|---|---|---|-------|-----|--------|---|---|---|---|---|
| | | ♪ | snare | 10 | Yamaha S | snare | | snare | | snare |
| | | ♪ | kick | 10 | Yamaha S | kick | | kick | | kick |
| | | ♪ | hi-hat | 10 | Yamaha S | hi-hat | | hi-hat | | hi-hat |

separately. Similarly you could record two different piano parts on different tracks and allocate them the same MIDI channel because they are using the same instrument.

In the arrange window you can literally arrange your music. This is done by cutting up and moving the blocks of data around, or copying and pasting them. For instance, I only recorded four bars of the drum parts, I then copied and pasted them into the next four bars and so on (Figure 3.2).

The arrange window is also where you would usually do your recording. Providing you have a MIDI input device, like a keyboard, attached to your PC through a MIDI interface, and the MIDI inputs are enabled in the software, then you should be able to record straight into the program. Most sequencers have some sort of indicator showing MIDI activity. In the Cubase example the transport bar (the graphic with the play and record buttons on) has a MIDI IN and MIDI OUT LED which flashes when MIDI moves through the program. So if you hit the keys on your keyboard the lights should flash. If not then you may need to do a little more setting up before you can record anything.

So, to record a live MIDI performance here's what you do:

1 Select a track for recording.
2 Give the track a MIDI channel and an output port.
3 Set the tempo and turn the metronome on or off depending if you need it.
4 Press record on the transport bar.
5 Play with your entire soul.
6 Press stop when you've finished.

A block should now have appeared alongside the track you were recording onto. Fantastic! you're now recording your own music, soon you'll be a star. Now let's copy and paste that block onto another track. If we give it a different MIDI channel we should be able to get the two tracks to play back together with different instrument sounds.

**How do you select the sound you want?**

Well each MIDI instrument has an address which consists of two numbers; Bank and Program (also called patch). The arrange page will give you a place where you can specify these numbers for each track. Consult the documentation of your MIDI device or soundcard to find out which instruments these numbers refer to.

So far we've managed to record something and maybe you've even moved blocks of stuff around the screen but we haven't been able to actually edit any notes that we played. Also, if you don't play an instrument or you have no MIDI input device then so far you've recorded nothing either. Let's get into the first of a MIDI sequencer's editing pages to see what can be done about all that.

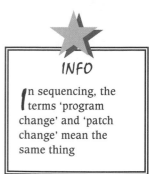

**INFO**

*In sequencing, the terms 'program change' and 'patch change' mean the same thing*

## Piano roll editor

This is also known as 'Key edit', 'Matrix editor', or just plain 'edit', but 'piano roll' is the most descriptively accurate term because that's what it looks like, a piano roll. What's a piano roll? Oh come on, it's a long roll of paper with holes punched in it to tell an old automatic piano what to play, like you see in old western movies. Anyway, a piano roll editor looks a bit like Figure 3.3 (it's from Cubase again because they claim to be the first people to have used it).

Down the left hand side you can see a representation of a piano keyboard. Along the top is the same timebase as found in the arrange page. In the main window lies a grid, the axes of which

Figure 3.3 Cubase VST key edit window

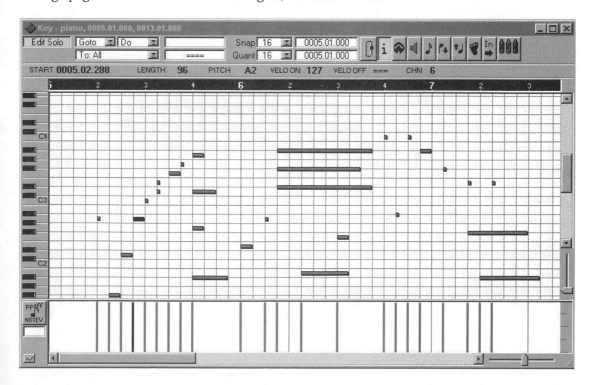

correspond to pitch and time. The dots shown represent the notes which have been recorded. The height of each dot denotes its pitch relative to the keyboard on the left. Its horizontal position shows its start point (when the note was struck) and its length shows how long the note was held.

So, you can easily see if you played a wrong note. You can then pick up the corresponding dot and move it to the correct position. You can copy and paste, and delete or whatever you want. You can also add notes by using a pencil tool. So if you can't play a keyboard, this is where you can enter notes.

A handy variation of the piano roll editor has come about in the form of the drum grid editor. This is very similar but has a list of drum sounds down the left in place of the piano keyboard. The grid is usually tighter because note length isn't as important with percussive instruments. This has made drum programming far easier to cope with.

## MIDI controllers

The graphic editing of MIDI controllers makes adding events like pitch bend, modulation, volume, filtering, an absolute doddle.

Controller editing is usually done in the piano roll window. This makes it easy to see which notes you are applying the control to.

In the example from Cakewalk (Figure 3.4), the bottom half of the window is showing the 'velocity' controller values. It refers to the starting velocity (how hard the note was struck) of each note. The velocity can be any one of 128 values (0-127), shown at the side. I have drawn in a rather obvious fade in and out. You can see that the notes in bar 1 were hit with increasing velocity, in bar 2, the velocity gets softer. In the same way, I could draw in a pitch bend.

INFO

*A*s you get deeper into the wonders of MIDI and how to apply it to different devices, this ability to draw on controllers becomes a wonderful tool to make your sequences more interesting.

Figure 3.4 Twelve Tone's Cakewalk showing notes (top half) and velocity controller values (bottom half)

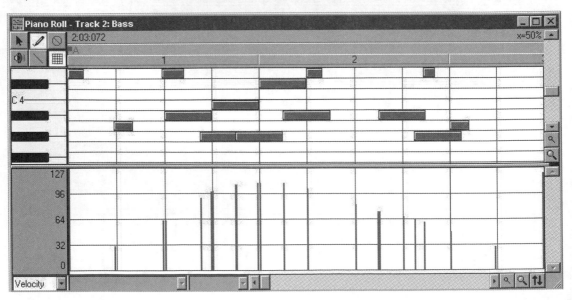

## Event list editor

Every time a piece of MIDI data is generated, by striking a key, moving the pitch wheel, or pushing a button etc. it is called a MIDI *event*. A sequencer usually allows these events to be edited directly. This is a little hard-core for most people but it can be very handy for putting in controller data, patch changes and stuff, and it's also a good way of finding out what MIDI information is actually going on.

An event list simply lists all the MIDI events in time order. Figure 3.5 is part of the event list from a track in Logic Audio. It shows the information about each event, starting with 'position' in bars, 'status' or which sort of MIDI event, 'cha' MIDI channel, 'num' a number relevant to the MIDI event, usually note number or bank number, 'val' a value relative to the number, and 'length/info' which gives note length or other information.

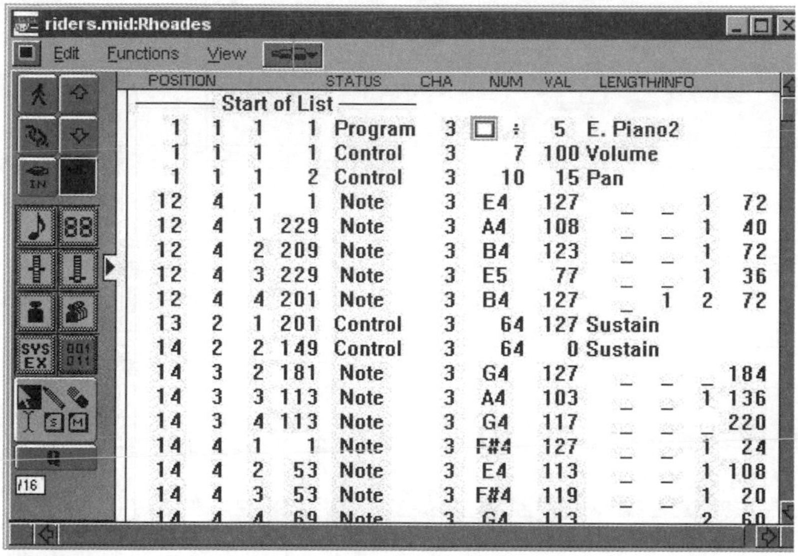

Figure 3.5 Event list in Emagic Logic Audio

So, going through the list we can see that the first event is a program change. This tells the output MIDI device which instrument to select. On this occasion it's patch number 5 which happens to be Electric Piano 2. Then we have two MIDI controller events, one setting up the volume of the instrument, the other setting the instrument's stereo position. The first note doesn't occur until bar 12 and we are given information on the note played (E4), its velocity (127) and its length. Later on there are a couple of events for controlling sustain on notes.

Any and every MIDI event will be listed here. They can be edited and added to and deleted. It's not a very musical part of sequencing but it can be useful for fine-tuning your sequences.

### INFO

Some people are known to use the event list editor for entering and editing all the notes, but then some people are brushed with madness.

**INFO**

If scoring is your main goal in PC based music making, check out Chapter 7 on Notation (page 38).

## Score editor

The information contained in a MIDI note event is mainly pitch and length. It's not very hard then to translate that information onto the musical stave

Most sequencers contain some form of score editing. Some just give you the option to print out the score, others allow you to edit notes directly on the stave, add dynamic markings, titles, lyrics, tablature and finally print out your score in a brilliantly desk-top-published kind of way. Most are somewhere in-between.

If you can read music then this could be a useful editing tool, otherwise it may be nice to have a printed score of your creation so that other people could play it. You can move notes about, add notes, delete, cut and paste, all the usual stuff, and print out.

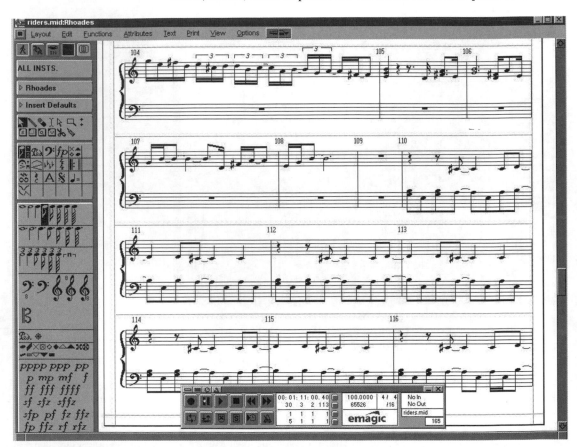

Figure 3.6 the score editor in Emagic's Logic Audio

A dedicated notation package usually contains the best score writing tools. Some sequencers have excellent scoring facilities but rarely come up to the standard of the full-on, professional, scoring package.

# Hard disk recording

# 4

**S**oftware hard disk recording is one of the more recent advances in recording technology. As processing power has increased over the last couple of years, the potential of hard disk recording has exploded, with major advances and updates being made every six months or so. Previously the toys of the rich and famous, the power of the standard PC has brought professional quality recording to the home user for an increasingly affordable investment.

There are a few interchangeable terms here: hard disk recording package/program/system; audio sequencer; multitrack audio software. All of them mean the same thing – a computer based software system for recording onto hard disk.

Hard disk recording was initially a hardware thing. Chunky rack-mountable units with internal hard drives, designed to replace the standard analogue, open reel, tape based multitracker. This is still an easy and professional solution without all that mucking about with computers. Computers were already involved in the recording

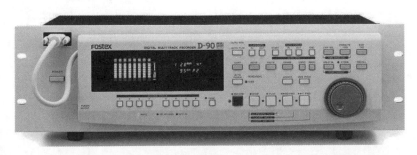

Figure 4.1 Fostex D90 hard disk recorder

Figure 4.2 Soundscape's PC
based system

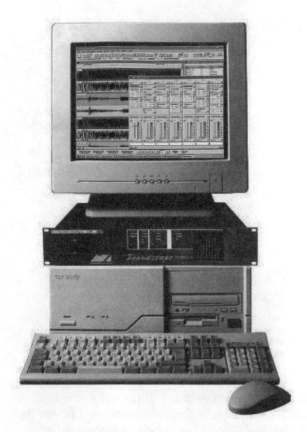

process as sequencers and it wasn't long before they were
connected to the hard disk recorders as control devices and editors.

The problem at this stage was that the computer power couldn't
really cope with the amount of data generated by recording and
editing multiple tracks of audio. The audio inputs and outputs on
computers were also rubbish (still are in many cases) and so, until
technology brought them up to scratch, recording onto computers
wasn't really a viable option.

Two main companies saw the potential of a computer based hard
disk recording system from early on, Digidesign and Soundscape.
They used dedicated hardware with external hard disks and custom
made, high quality, inputs and outputs. This took most of the
processing away from the computer in order to circumnavigate the
limitations. The computers were used as the control centre and
editing suite. These two companies still produce the most
professional software and hardware based recording systems.

So when do the rest of us get a look in? Well, what everyone
wanted was a whole studio on their PC. Not just sequencing but
also the ability to record real sound, vocal tracks, guitar tracks, and
all for under the price of a decent four track tape based
multitracker.

The sequencer software companies began to aim for this ideal

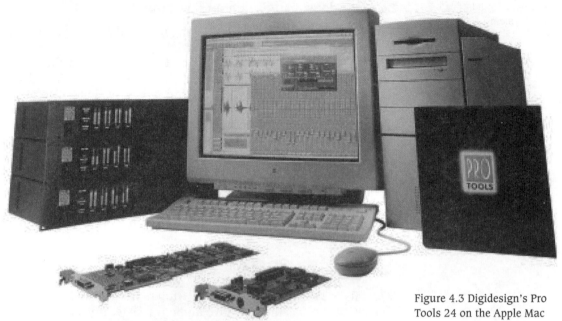

Figure 4.3 Digidesign's Pro Tools 24 on the Apple Mac

and along with advances in processing power came integrated four track, then eight track systems using a computer's internal hard disk. The quality of soundcards improved and some hardware manufacturers began producing soundcards expressly for audio recording. A fully working studio on a PC, for a few hundred quid, was only a matter of time.

Today, it's here. It can be a little flaky at times, but improvements are being made all the time. In the last year we have seen eight track audio soar to virtually unlimited tracks. Dynamics processing giving real-time equalisation on individual tracks, the adding of real-time effects such as delay, chorus and reverb. Hardware audio cards giving eight ins and outputs with proper professional connectors, for reasonable money. It's getting better and cheaper all the time.

## That's the history lesson, but what can you actually do with it?

Hard disk recording is about recording multiple tracks of audio onto hard disk – simple. Its concept is identical to that of tape. In a musical situation you record each instrument onto a separate track. Once recorded you can play the tracks back together and adjust the volume of each track until you get the correct 'mix' of sound. You can edit each track individually, add effects and other dynamic processing and also position, or pan, the track in the stereo field.

## So what does a studio on a PC contain?

Well, first thing you need is something to record onto, that'll be the hard disk. There will be a software mixing desk to allow you to alter levels. Effects (FX) boxes allowing you to add reverb and chorus etc. to individual tracks. Equalisation (EQ), these are like treble and bass controls on an amp, but on individual tracks. Some kind of sound or audio card to allow for real inputs and outputs.

That's the basis of your studio. Digital recording also allows for all sorts of editing not really possible with tape, like copy and paste, normalisation and looping.

Let's have a look at the software. You can get dedicated hard disk recording software but the most popular ones are those which are integrated into a MIDI sequencer, and that's what I'll use as examples.

## The Arrange Window

Yep, this is exactly the same as the arrange window in a MIDI sequencer, but this time we have audio tracks recorded alongside MIDI tracks (Figure 4.4).

The layout should be familiar but now we can see seven audio tracks in the arrange window as well as a couple of MIDI tracks.

Figure 4.4 The Arrange Window in Emagic's Logic Audio Gold

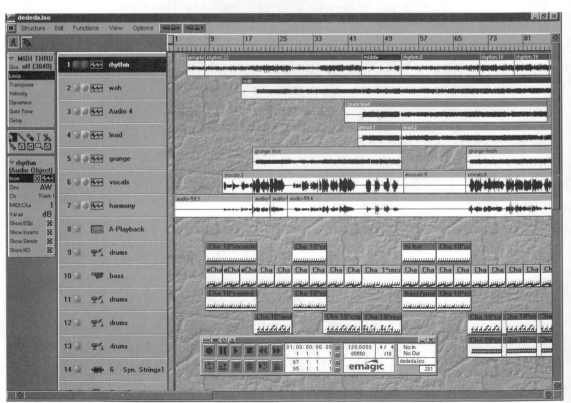

The audio tracks are visually represented by blocks, as the MIDI is, but you can see in these blocks what looks like a mess of black stuff. This is a graphical representation of amplitude (volume) over time of the audio track – like what you might have seen on an oscilloscope at school. This is how an audio file is usually portrayed.

The same editing rules apply in this page as they did to the MIDI blocks. You can copy and paste them and move them around, as long as they remain on an audio track, MIDI and audio are not interchangeable. On track one, named rhythm, you can see at the end I have copy and pasted the last few bars a couple of times. That's kind of handy, because I wanted to lengthen the song and rather than recording the track again, or recording an extra bit, I just repeated the last few bars – easy.

You soon find that you don't actually have to play everything right all the time. If you record one or two takes of a guitar track you'll probably find that you have enough 'right' bits to make one good track. For example, you've got a complicated riff going through each verse but it's really hard to play. You record yourself playing the riff for a couple of minutes, pick out the one that sounded the best and paste it throughout the whole song. Hardly rock and roll but who's going to notice, besides you can leave all that practising stuff for when you're booked to play Wembley.

> ### INFO
>
> That's the beauty of digital recording, it's so easy to change and rearrange songs, saves so much time. That time is usually taken up by all the constant mucking about you find yourself doing to tracks, just because you can.

## The mixer

Okay, so where's this mixer you talked about?. Figure 4.5 shows Logic Audio's mixing environment (as they call it). The audio environment has faders for track volume, panning controls, 'sends' for routing out to busses, 'inserts' for FX and EQ, everything an analogue desk has, but more. It's also MIDI controllable which means that every function of this mixer has a MIDI address and can be controlled by the usual MIDI functions. You can literally draw

Figure 4.5 The mixing environment in Emagic's Logic Audio Gold

controller information onto a track to control volume, panning, anything you like. You want to fade in a track while fading out another, impossible to do with a mouse, so you draw each movement in as a MIDI controller and the mixer moves by itself.

## Effects

All right then, how about adding all those FXs and EQ that make a recording into a gorgeous piece of music?

The advent of 'real-time' processing is what has allowed the PC as a digital recorder to evolve into a virtual studio. Previously to add a delay to an audio track you would have to select the timing and feedback, process that onto the waveform and then, finally, you could hear it back. If it wasn't what you wanted you would have to undo the operation and try again until you got it right, which is a right pain. 'Real-time' means that you can apply an effect directly on a track and alter the parameters while the track is playing. So altering the delay time is simply a matter of moving a knob or slider and you get an immediate response – no more guessing. In the Logic example the FX and EQ are accessible directly from the mixer. In Cubase VST the FX and EQ have their own windows, using graphics to mimic the look of its real life counterpart (Figure 4.6).

Figure 4.6 Steinberg's Cubase VST mixer, FX and EQ windows

The effects used in these programs require a great deal of processing power as they are overlaid on the audio rather than actually transforming the audio file to create the effect. This means that the effect can be added or removed without destructively editing the actual audio file.

So, does it feel like a studio yet? You've got a mixing desk, you've got fully parametric EQ, you've got a rack of useful effects, all on your PC. That's pretty amazing really.

## Audio track editing

Recording stuff, adding effects and mixing it down is all very well but it's hardly taking advantage of what the hard disk has to offer over tape in the way of editing.

All hard disk recording packages offer limited audio editing facilities. For more intense, full-on editing you need to get a dedicated piece of software as described in the next chapter. These can often be used within an audio sequencer, but for now we'll look at the basic functions found in most programs.

Audio editing is applying destructive edits directly onto the waveform (some packages have multiple 'undo' functions which means you can restore the waveform to its original state even after you've edited it to destruction, this can be called non-destructive

Figure 4.7 Audio track editing in Emagic's Logic Audio Gold

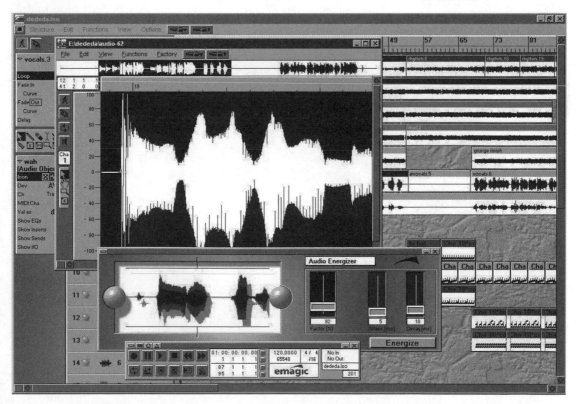

editing). This enables you to fine-tune the recorded audio. It may be the removal of accidental noises or background noise, cutting off unwanted bits, applying fades, copying and pasting more precisely than in the arrange window. Or it may be applying odd effects, experimentation is the key here.

The usual functions found in this editor are:

**Normalisation**: averages out the volume across the piece of audio.

**Fade in/out**

**Reverse**

**DC offset**: sometimes in digital recording the audio can be off-centred and can cause digital noise, this function allows you to offset it away from distortion.

**Change gain**: boosting or attenuating the overall volume.

**Invert**: inverting a waveform to prevent, or cause phase shifting.

**Silence**: removes a piece of audio and leaves silence.

**Trim**: removes any audio around that which has been highlighted.

Figure 4.8 The application of a fade in Cakewalk Pro Audio.

These functions may not make complete sense to you now, but will become more important as you become experienced in hard disk recording. Most are obvious though, like fade in/out.

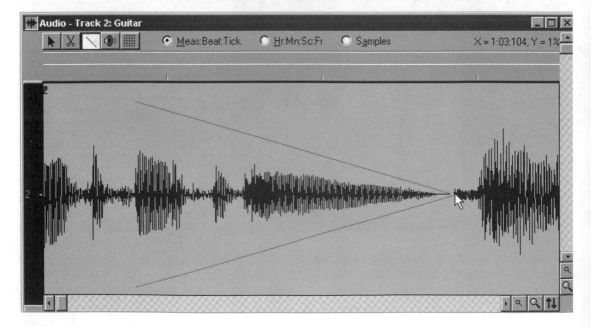

# Pitch shift and time stretching

Everybody wants to do this and it is a very clever thing that is only possible within the digital domain. In a sampler if you play a note higher than the original sample, it is speeded up to reach that pitch. It's like spinning a vinyl record too fast. To change the pitch of a digital audio track you could speed it up but then it would no longer fit in time to the other tracks. Or if you wanted to slow the whole song down everything would reduce in pitch. This is not really what we want. So, we have to find a way of separating the two and applying each independently.

Again, the clever programming people came up with some algorithms (or sets of instructions) which allow this to happen – up to a point.

### So, what's this pitch/time stuff about?

You've recorded a vocal track and you'd like to add harmonies. Great, rather than try to sing them you could make a copy of the track and pitch shift it up a fifth to create instant harmonies. Incredibly you can keep the timing the same.

Alternatively you've got two drum loops you want to use but they are recorded at different bpm (beats per minute). You can stretch one to fit the other without lowering the pitch.

This all sounds very easy but it's a hard thing to do convincingly. Go 20% either way and the audio may begin to lose its integrity because the computer is doing a lot of guess work at filling in holes or applying harmonic correction to prevent the 'pinky and perky' effect.

The simplest use of these tools is for correcting timing and adjusting flat notes. Creating harmonies can be very convincing as long as you don't go too far from the original, and time stretching is most effective on drum loops where pitch is less important. This technology is advancing all the time and just keeps getting better.

# Summary

Hard disk recording is a fabulous thing. It gives the user so much power and new possibilities in creativity right in your own home.

The ability to record and mix music is all very well, but to do it well is a skill. Sound engineers train for years before they are good enough to produce really professional sounding albums. They work their way up from making the tea in a studio, spending time learning the recording process, the gear, the way other people work. You can't do it overnight, it takes time and patience, so don't expect your music to suddenly sound of releasable quality. That's why studios cost money to hire, it's not just the equipment, it's the geezer who knows how to work it.

It's not all doom and gloom though. Have a go, see what happens, there's no reason why you can't produce something which sounds half decent. It'll sound a hell of a lot better than the recordings you made on that old tape machine.

*Sample/wave editing* **5**

 his is hard disk recording again in as much as the program allows you to record to hard disk, but it is more often used to edit audio that has already been recorded, in greater depth than an audio sequencer.

### So, what are the advantages or differences?

This is mainly to do with speed, accuracy and quality. Wave editing packages are designed to deal with very large audio files, they are offering, in effect, a mastering suite. It's a place (or in this case a program) where you can apply the finishing touches to a piece of audio, or completely re-edit it, before burning it onto a CD (or record it to cassette if you like, but I am trying to keep it hi-tech here).

Non-musical applications would be in the form of voice editing, sound effects or Foley editing, soundtrack editing for film, sound analysis and restoration and so on.

You may have recorded a lecture on DAT. You could dump it into your PC and edit out the coughs or the irrelevant bits, remove background noise and equal out the level.

You may have a bunch of sound effect samples you need to add to a piece of video. You could paste these effects along a time line to match up exactly to the frames of the video.

On a musical level it could be used simply to edit a track within a song, or for mastering the finished stereo wavefile produced by the audio sequencer. Adding frequency enhancements, final EQ and FX, trimming the audio to the exact length and applying P&Q information for burning to CD.

### INFO

*F*oley editing is another term for sound effects, named after a Mr Foley who generated live sound effects for radio plays.

Figure 5.1 Sonic Foundry's
Sound Forge

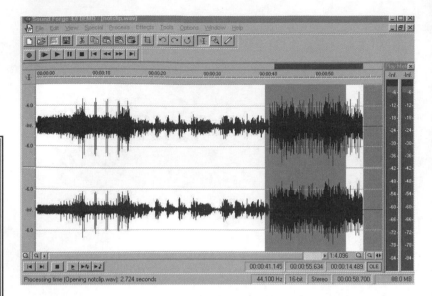

## INFO

**Y**ou may find the
editing functions
on a hardware sampler
limiting. You could
dump the sample into
the PC and edit it, find
loop points etc. far
more accurately, and
then dump it back.

The frequency analysis of one of my recorded songs (Figure 5.2)
shows some low frequency sound (in black) at around the 20Hz
mark. I didn't record any sounds that low so it's probably noise or
interference. Now I know it's there I can remove it by applying a
high-pass filter. I may not be able to hear it during the song, but
someone else might, and the analysis has enabled me to identify it
and remove it – cool.

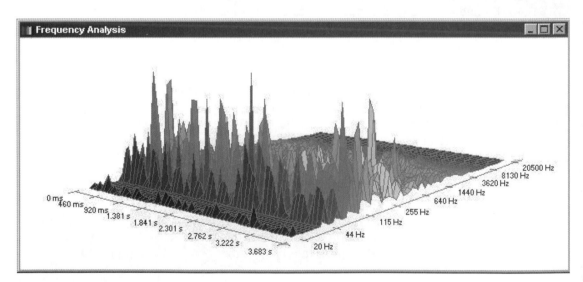

Figure 5.2 Frequency
analysis of a song using
Steinberg's Wavelab

# Plug-ins 6

This is a great idea and goes a long way to eliminating the need for outboard equipment.

You may already be familiar with the idea of 'plug-in' filters for graphic programs or for an internet browser. A plug-in is an additional piece of software which will only function within another piece of software. It literally plugs into a program to give further facilities.

Hard disk recording plug-ins are often software simulations of 'real-life' pieces of studio hardware. Compressors, enhancers, noise reduction, parametric EQ, reverb, multi-effects, are among the plug-ins available. What they do is give you the quality and controls of a real compressor etc. in software form. So instead of shelling out a couple of grand for a Focusrite Red valve compressor you could get the plug-in version and pay about a quarter of the price. Does it sound the same as the real thing? Well, kind of, it's pretty close and is certainly a good add-on to a hard disk recording package.

Some plug-ins were created expressly as software and can add some very high quality processing to your music.

The reverbs that come with some audio sequencers are usually okay, but not much better than that. To improve the quality you could get a third party reverb plug-in.

One particular plug-in that has been around a while is Antare's Auto-Tune. It's a fascinating piece of software that automatically shifts the pitch of a track onto the correct notes of a predefined scale. In reality this means that if you whack it onto a vocal track,

Figure 6.1 Steinberg's Red
Valve-It plug-in recreates the
warmth of valve technology
and allows the user to select
different amplifier
simulations. So you want
your guitar to sound like it
was played through a
Marshall stack? No problem.

**ODD FACT**

Professionals seem to like to pay a lot of money for their gear, it makes them feel 'professional', even if it comes on a single floppy disk.

the singer will instantly be singing in tune no matter how bad they are. Pop stars don't like to talk about it, but you will find it's used on a massive number of chart records.

Until recently plug-ins were written specifically for a single program. The advent of 'DirectX' within Windows 95 has allowed third party developers to write software to be used by any audio sequencer which supports DirectX, ending incompatibility annoyances.

Plug-ins usually cost a lot more than you think, often matching or passing the price of your audio sequencer. You are paying for a great deal of research, development, and the resultant quality.

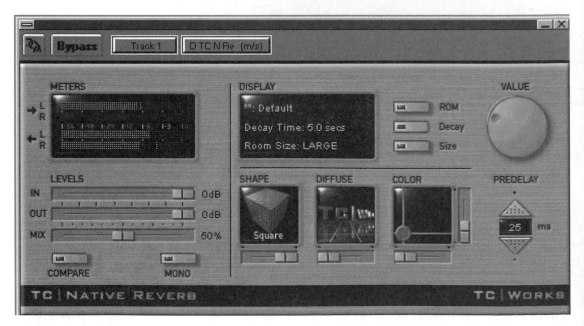

Figure 6.2 TC Electronic's
Native Reverb

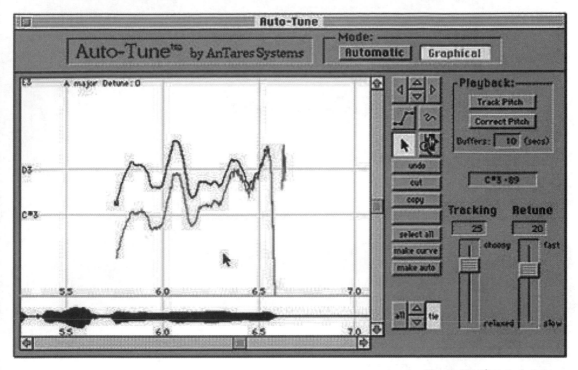

Figure 6.3 Altare's Autotune automatically shifts the pitch of a track onto the correct notes of a predefined scale

# 7 ★

# Notation and score writing

**T**hrough MIDI, publishing music has become simple and impressive. No longer do you have to sit at a piano for hours, playing the same phrase over and over while you put marks on a sheet of manuscript. Connect a MIDI keyboard to you PC, play ... and gasp as your whole performance is transcribed instantly.

Even those who can write music off the top of their heads can now put dots on the screen and get an instant playback of what they've composed.

It is possible to do full orchestral scoring, 64 staves, and print out a full score as well as individual parts. Text and markings can be added and the layout of the score edited in order to get the print-out you are after.

MIDI functionality can often be applied to the same extent as a MIDI sequencer. Controller information can be put onto the stave to correspond to the written dynamics. So when the score says 'p' for 'piano' then there is a corresponding reduction in MIDI volume. With this kind of control you can get a reasonably accurate performance on playback using the PC's soundcard or an external MIDI module. The composer no longer has to hire an orchestra in order to get an idea of what his music will sound like. Although I'd advise that it would be worth investing in a decent MIDI device for playback so that the orchestra sounds are as realistic as possible. There's nothing worse than writing a piece of music for a string quartet that sounds fantastic in your head, and then have it crucified by rubbish sounds from your soundcard.

## But don't you have to be a very accurate player to get decent results?

Well, yes to a degree, the more accurate your playing the less editing you'll have to do afterwards. The more professional programs do have the ability to cope with sloppy playing rather well. Sibelius (a top end notation program) will sense variations in tempo and adapt accordingly. Other programs use a footswitch to dictate the tempo so you can vary as much as you like.

It's the time factor that's most impressive. Anyone who writes musical scores for ensembles containing transposing instruments knows how long it can take to transpose the music for all the instruments. With software it's easy. You can pick an instrument and key from a defined list and the computer will transpose everything for you instantly. Once you've completed the whole score you can extract parts individually and print them out for each musician.

Figure 7.1 Sibelius – the guvnor notation program

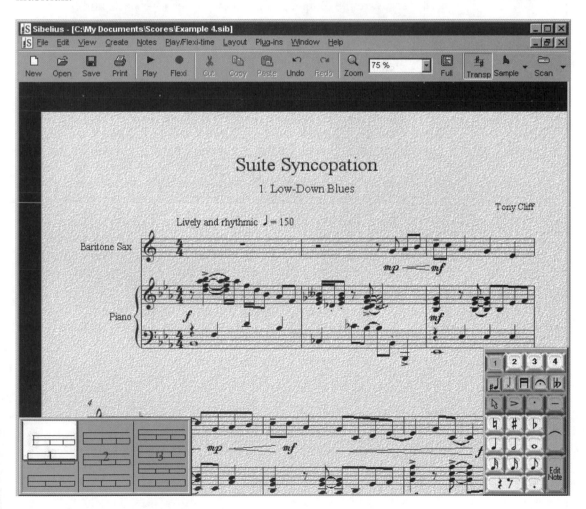

Percussion notation and guitar tabulature can all be included with the relevant note heads and markings, as well as guitar chord symbols and fret diagrams.

It's also a great tool for those of you who don't read music but may need to publish the score so that other people can play your creations. MIDI files from sequencer programs can be imported and edited, each track being given its own staff and track names would be retained. You also might just learn something.

Adding lyrics is also a doddle. As you type, the words and syllables automatically arrange themselves under the notes and hyphenate accordingly.

Educational applications are obvious. A student can see instantly how notation relates to the keys being played as the notes appear on the monitor. Complicated pieces of music can be slowed down and played along with, making it easier to learn. Practising with a full orchestra is not an option for everyone, but with notation software the computer could play all the other parts and turn the page (metaphorically speaking) as you play along.

**INFO**

Most companies who produce notation software offer some form of educational discount so that even impoverished students and teachers can get access to professional scoring software.

## Scanning

A recent advance in scoring technology is that of scanning. Optical character recognition (OCR) has got to the stage where a piece of manuscript can be scanned into the computer and the individual notes are recognised by the program. So you can now scan in an old piece of music and get the computer to play it back. Or you could transpose the scanned piece of music, print it out, and give it to your trombone player. You could even archive old manuscripts (after making any copyright considerations) and print them out at your leisure.

Notation software does for written music what word processing did for typing. With the technology of printers always increasing, the quality of print out is instantly publishable. It's never been quicker or easier to work on your masterpiece.

# *Software synthesis* 8

So you've got your studio and your MIDI sequencer set up on your PC, and it's the control centre, the brain that's controlling all your synthesisers and samplers. Hang on, why do I have all this external hardware cluttering up the place, surely my computer can create it's own sound without the need for all this hardware?

Okay, why not. Let's enter the world of software synthesis. This is a relatively new and blossoming area of PC music. It's full of possibilities and potential, hampered only by the huge requirements in processing power to manage the feat. Create a computer model of a hardware sound module or synthesiser and access it directly on screen. Seems logical enough.

Both Roland and Yamaha have launched attempts at the software synth. Roland's Virtual Sound Canvas is based upon their popular Sound Canvas series of GS modules. Yamaha based their S-Y soft-synth on their MU range of sound modules and have now released S-YXG soft-synths to model the popular XG format Yamaha has been using as a standard General MIDI variation throughout their recent range of synths.

The quality of the first releases were surprisingly good but were both plagued with the same, rather fundamental, problem. The response time to real-time MIDI input was rubbish. What does that mean? Simply, with the Roland Virtual Sound Canvas, as an example, you would hit a note on your MIDI keyboard and anything up to a couple of seconds later you would hear the sound. Obviously this made live performance impossible. The soft-synths were

**INFO**

A version of the Virtual Sound Canvas will be included in the second release of Windows 98 and also Quicktime version 3, which means that everyone will have a half decent set of GM sounds on their PC (or Mac) as standard ... which is nice.

carefully marketed as 'playback only' synths which meant that they were fine at playing back MIDI files or sequencers, because the initial delay wouldn't really matter. The plus side of these synths was things like the massive amounts of polyphony made available.

These problems have largely been overcome by increases in processing power as well as improvements in the software. You'll often find simple software synthesisers accompanying soundcards, enhancing the quality and polyphony of the on board synth. These can work very well although they have no editing possibilities and lack the quality of hardware synths. In time, software versions of sound modules and synthesisers will be as usable as their hardware counterparts.

## Analogue modular synthesis

Running in parallel with Roland and Yamaha's development of software sound modules has been the computer modelling of analogue synthesis. There has been a massive return to the 'feel' and sound of analogue synthesisers which disappeared for a number of years when digital synthesis arrived with the Yamaha DX7. This has been largely driven by the dance music industry, whose artists demand fat bass lines, and strange electronic noises with instant real-time control by fiddling with knobs.

Analogue synthesis is sound generation in its purest form. It begins with a simple waveform generator (or oscillator) which produces a sawtooth or square wave. Next you could apply a filter which would highlight various frequencies and alter the tone of the sound. You could then apply a modulator, a low frequency oscillator (LFO), which could be applied to the frequency (pitch) or amplitude (volume) of the sound to create vibrato or tremolo effects. An envelope generator (ADSR) could be used to shape the sound over time, changing the *attack* (how quickly the sound reaches its full volume), the *decay* (the rate at which the sound falls away), *sustain* (how far the note continues while the key is held down), and *release* (sustain after the key is released).

There are many more 'modules' like the ones described which are used in analogue synthesis. This is often called 'modular synthesis' because of the use of different modules to create and alter the sound.

Why am I telling you all this? This simplified description of analogue synthesis hopefully helps you to understand how logically easy it is to model these simple modules on a computer. Examples of this kind of soft-synth have been around for a while, usually the product of university research students, and have been interesting but not very usable.

The breakthrough came from a bunch of dance music enthusiasts and programmers calling themselves the 'Propellerheads'. It took

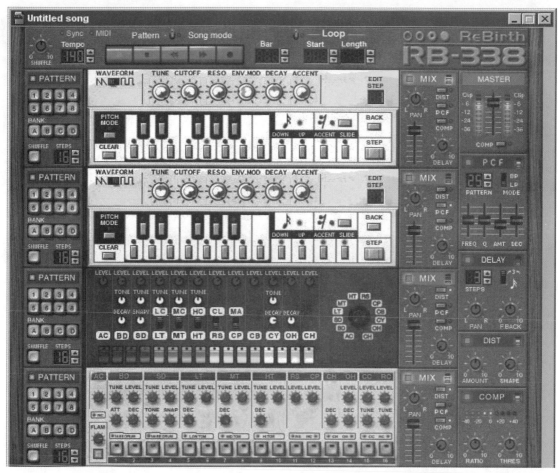

Figure 8.1 Propellerhead's Rebirth RB338 V2

everyone by surprise except Steinberg (creators of Cubase) who grabbed it and marketed it to great success. The program is called ReBirth RB-338.

ReBirth is a stunning computer model of two classic Roland analogue synths – the MC303, a monophonic synth with a built in step sequencer, and the TR808 drum machine. The current version (V2) now includes a TR909 as well. These are the staple diet sounds of dance and techno music and the accuracy of the sounds generated by this program are astounding. The graphical interface works in the same way as the original, a few extras tagged on like delay and distortion, and the inclusion of two MC303's was a master stroke. It's very easy to use, instantly gratifying and doesn't rely on MIDI input for triggering.

Initially ReBirth was a self contained program, not designed to run in conjunction with anything else. Now later versions allow it to be integrated and synchronised into MIDI sequencers so you can write other music alongside.

The success and beauty of ReBirth has spawned a stack of

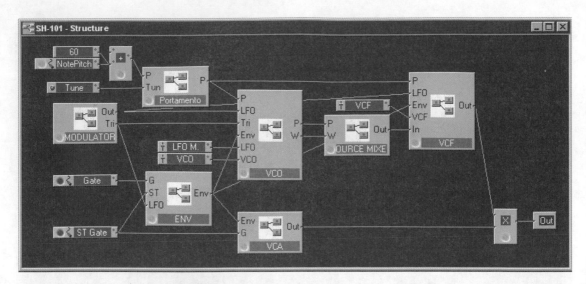

Figure 8.2 Native
Instrument's Generator
needs a good spec PC

software modular synths which are just becoming available. One
which takes the whole idea of 'modular' very seriously is Native
Instruments 'Generator' (Figure 8.2). It gives the user a blank page
and a set of module building blocks. You can choose how you
connect things together, what bits affect other bits, just like the
original modular synths. This time we have polyphony and full
MIDI control. Unfortunately we start to see response time problems
on lower specification computers, so a fast PC will be important.

Software sampling is another area I mentioned briefly in an
earlier chapter. This has become a reality with the 'GigaSampler'
from Nemesys (Figure 8.3). It claims to dispense with the need for a
hardware sampler, offering all the functionality and anything up to
2GB of space for samples (hardware samplers typically can manage
128MB of sample RAM) The GigaSampler uses hard disk space to
store the samples, sucking them into system RAM for triggering via
MIDI.

It's early days yet and few home users will have the stupidly fast
computer needed to get the most out of the software. It's still a very
impressive piece of programming.

There are loads of pieces of software around that utilise sample
playback as their sound source. Most of these are in the form of
drum machines and loop playing devices. None of this involves
triggering via MIDI it's just picking up little samples and throwing
them onto a grid. Minutes of fun can be had creating top dance
tunes using drum loops and bass samples. An actually quite good
example would be Steinberg's BBOX which looks like a simplified
version of Rebirth with a single TR808 style interface. What makes
this one good is that it comes pack with fantastic samples of old
drum machines, the 808 and 909 of course but also Linn Drum,
Simmons, Korg Mini Pop's and all sorts of old favourites.

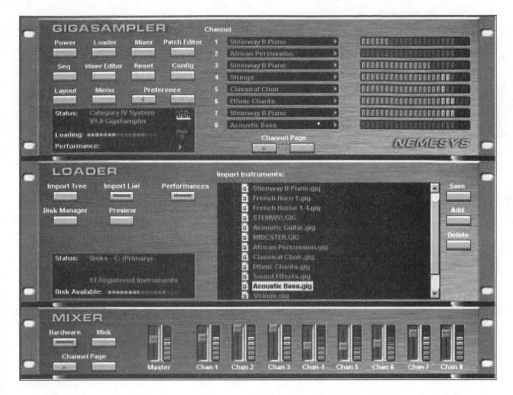

Another deceptively brilliant sample based program is Sonic Foundry's ACID. This program allows you to drop in tracks using different loops to create music. The clever bit is that it automatically time stretches so that the timing of each loop matches up. You can also pitch shift independently so that all the music is in tune. It does it all so well that it's worth the price just for the time stretch/pitch shift ability. Somehow it makes music creation far too easy.

Figure 8.3 Nemesys' GigaSampler

## Virtual acoustic modelling

A new advance from Yamaha has been with their acclaimed Virtual Acoustic Modelling technology found in their VL range of synthesisers. This is a new form of synthesis using computer models of acoustical environments to generate incredibly life-like sounds and very strange new sounds. An example would be that the computer holds a model of all the acoustical properties of a wind instrument, how the air vibrates, the effect of the instrument's material. Apply to this a similar model of a bowed string instrument and the result would be an accurate representation of a bowed flute, if such a thing was possible. The possibilities of sound creation are limitless. Originally only available in their hardware units, Yamaha are now releasing a software version (Figure 8.4). Again, a high flying PC is recommended.

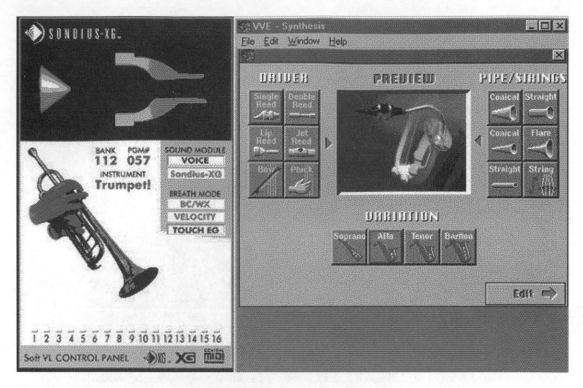

Figure 8.4 Yamaha's Soft VL

## Knobs or not?

These kinds of software are seen by many as the future of synthesis. You'll have sound modules, synthesisers, samplers, all on screen, all on hard disk. Hmmm. I have some reservations about this.

In the late 1980's when digital synths became smooth, black slabs, with two buttons and a horribly complicated, page based, editing system on a small screen, people went searching for the old analogue synths in pure frustration. They wanted tactile interaction, knobs and sliders to move which responded immediately. Editing which was obvious and easy. Modern synths are again covered which such knobs in response to these demands. So, taking all that hardware we love fiddling with and dumping it onto a computer controlled by a single mouse, seems a little foolish to me. One of the biggest complaints against ReBirth is that you can only move a single control at a time. In response new MIDI controllers, bits of hardware with knobs on that send out MIDI controller information, have been designed to work with computer based synths, so you can now fiddle with real knobs in ReBirth. This is a great development but you are back to having a load of external gear again.

## PC power

My other concern is that each of these programs requires a serious
PC to run well. You will probably want to run a couple of synths as
well as a sampler alongside your audio sequencer, which is running
multiple tracks of audio with plug-in effects. Considering that the
PC struggles just to keep the audio sequencer glitch free, running all
these other processor and memory hungry programs would probably
make your PC catch fire. As processing power increases then, of
course, this shouldn't be a problem. Maybe. As it seems to be going
at the moment, software is ahead of the hardware by about six
months. By this I mean that you won't be able to get the best
performance out of the software you buy because it will be another
six months until a PC is created which is fast enough to achieve it.
When the technology catches up, the software suddenly requires a
whole new load of power to use the new advanced features, and so
it goes on.

One further thought. Hard drive failure. You've not just lost your
music, you've lost all your gear as well. Another thought. Don't
forget to back-up your work.

## So...

Reservations aside, software synthesis is reaching maturity and
offers many exciting features and quality for a lot less money that
the hardware counterpart. It's also good fun and can offer functions
that were never possible before.

# 9 *Internet music*

f ever there was a perpetually evolving technology then the internet is it. I am constantly surprised by new developments and it becomes increasingly hard to keep track. The beauty (although this beauty is fast being eroded by commercialism) is that the internet is (was) driven largely by enthusiasts, people with a passion for what they doing, a desire to be heard. The World Wide Web (WWW) is a global publishing house allowing the user to share their thoughts, ideas and their music with the world. No management required, no agents, no permission, no signed piece of paper. By putting your music on the web you become a published artist. Sounds good doesn't it?

## So, how does music relate to the internet?

Well, I'm not about to show you how to create html documents for publishing music, that information is freely available over the internet. What I will do is show you some of the tools being used and what they could mean for your music, that way if you wanted to have a go you would at least know what to look for and what is currently possible. Although, the use of 'currently' in this context refers to what's happening at the time of writing, by the time you actually read this then things may be rather different. It just means that the picture will hopefully be rosier than the one I'm 'currently' painting.

The first format of music to be shared over the internet was the MIDI file. A song created with a MIDI sequencer which can be played back through a MIDI device. MIDI files are very small, typically under 100kB and so are quick to download. Bulletin boards are filled with MIDI files of famous songs and original works. It's staggering how much work can go into those MIDI files of famous songs. The creator must spend hours working on the arrangement until every track is spot on the original. Others, it must be said, are appalling. Mind you, anyone attempting a MIDI file of *Pretty Vacant* by the Sex Pistols is on a hiding to nothing.

With General MIDI adopted by soundcards, the MIDI file you downloaded will sound pretty much as the writer intended. So, you write your MIDI music, post the file on the internet, and anyone with access can download and listen to your music through the synth on their own soundcard. Groovy. There is a niggling problem with this though, partly to do with your soundcard's synthesiser, and partly do to with ignorance. If you're a musician and you've got a couple of decent MIDI devices then your music will probably sound really good running through your quality synthesiser or whatever. When an adoring fan downloads the file they will hear it played back through their own soundcard, whose synthesiser is probably rubbish. So, although the music arrangement will sound as intended, the actually quality of the sounds will vary depending on the MIDI device being used for playback. Unfortunately many people are not aware of this and the listener may assume that what they are hearing is a real recording of your music, rather than a MIDI file playing through their own soundcard's synth. Subsequently they may tell you that your music is terrible for all the wrong reasons.

The next advance in internet MIDI files was to get the music to play directly off a web page, saving the listener from having to download and play the file themselves, well, we all like an easy life. This is where the internet music plug-in makes an appearance. The plug-in would interpret the MIDI information and route it to the soundcard without the user having to do anything. This way you could get music playing as soon as someone accessed your web page, and it would play in the background until they left. It's a great way to force people to listen to your music.

Samples have also been used in a small way. Short loops can be downloaded with the web page and told to repeat so that the surfer is treated to a bit of percussion as they browse the page. Other samples can be played as the mouse rolls over a link or active part of the page. This can be all very impressive and even humorous ... for about 2 minutes.

# Getting real songs onto the net

Mucking around with MIDI files and small samples is all very well but we want to publish real songs, recorded music, CD quality masterpieces. Of course you do, don't we all?

The problem is this: Audio files are huge in internet terms. A three minute stereo song at CD quality (16 bit/44.1kHz for those who've forgotten) is 30MB in size. If you consider that the usual amount of web space given away with a private dial-up internet account is around 10MB you can get an idea of what we're up against. Also consider the download time required for that amount of data. An average connection nowadays can give you a transfer rate of 3kB per second. 1MB would take several minutes to download, 30MB could take hours. Even the most devoted fan would go mad, not to mention broke, waiting that long for a download of a three minute song.

### The solution

The files must be smaller, not just smaller but at least a tenth of the size if not less. One way to reduce the file size is to reduce the quality. Drop down to 8 bit and your file halves, drop to 22kHz and it halves again. So, a 30MB file is now down to 7.5MB. Let's make it mono rather than stereo, halves again down to 3.75MB now that's almost acceptable in terms of download. One snag: your music suddenly sounds rubbish, the quality is now vastly reduced and sounds like something played on a battered old tape machine. We want CD quality, so what do we do?

This is where compression comes in. Now, compression in music recording terms is the process of reducing the dynamic range of an audio track so that loud sounds and soft sounds are reproduced at the same volume. Take a vocal track and compress it so that the screaming and the whispers are at the same volume. When it comes to compressing files on a computer this is very different although there are some similarities.

Most people should be familiar with file compression. When you install a piece of software it normally comes compressed on a floppy or CDROM. Installing the software 'unpacks' all the files and puts them on your hard drive. You may have also come across *.zip files which is a format where you can pack a load of files into a single smaller file which can be unpacked back to its original size. Can this be done to an audio file? Yes it can, but because audio files are single continuous files very little space is saved by compressing them in this format.

# MP3

So, is there any hope out there? Yes indeed. Some clever people have been working on the problem for some time and at the moment there seem to be two main players who have had any success. The first was the creation of the MP3 format. Using very clever compression software audio files could be reduced to a twelfth of their size with practically no reduction in quality. The compression process is irreversible and so an MP3 player is required to play back the file. All the software to compress and to listen to MP3's is freely available on the net so anyone can do it. The sound quality is remarkably good, so good in fact that the record industry fears loss of revenue through people putting copyrighted music into MP3 format and freely distributing it on the net.

## Copyright – theirs

It's all cool and groovy being able to get music free off the net, but if that music carries a copyright then you are breaking the law. Spare a thought for the artist who created it, struggling to pay back the advance he/she got from the record company. If you managed to get yourself signed then I imagine you wouldn't appreciate it much.

# Streaming audio

The other major player is a company called RealNetworks. Their RealAudio format has been around a while and has been responsible for improving the possibilities of music distribution on the internet. It uses a similar compression format to MP3 in that it can reduce the size of an audio file to a 15th of its original size with practically no loss of quality. Where RealAudio differs is in the ability to stream directly off the internet and play back in (almost) real time. Using the RealPlayer you can click on a music file and it begins to download. After a few seconds the file begins to play back while the rest is still downloading. Cool, no more hanging around waiting for a download. The latest version of the RealPlayer can also show embedded video and graphics at the same time. This is astonishing! So, I can get CD quality music and video streaming directly off the internet with no annoying download times!?!? Well, no actually you can't, not yet anyway. The speed of data transfer over the net is not nearly fast enough to cope with that sort of thing.

Consider your 3 minute, 30MB audio file, reduced with no loss of quality down to about 3MB. Download time is going to be anywhere between 10 – 30 minutes depending on your connection. Streaming it off the net doesn't increase the speed of download and so real time playback isn't going to happen. What you do get is 1 minute of downloading followed by 20 seconds of playback, followed by another minute of download, followed by another 20 seconds of playback and so on. You may as well download the whole thing and play it back afterwards.

It can work though. Either you have to get yourself a couple of serious ISDN lines to speed up your connection, or reduce the quality of the audio. Since few people have the money for ISDN reducing the quality is the only 'real' solution. So what's the result? Well, to get a constant stream off the internet the quality is reduced to sounding like music coming off a medium wave radio being held in a bath of water. Ho hum. It will get there though, just takes time for technology to provide the answers and increase the bandwidth.

## Quicktime 3

There is a newcomer to the streaming scene that has me suitably astonished. I only discovered it as I was putting the finishing touches to this book. Quicktime have come up with (or borrowed) an incredible compression format called the 'Qdesign codec'. You are probably familiar with Quicktime movies and the like, well, the new version, Quicktime 3, seems to have the capability of streaming near CD quality audio off a web page on a standard 28.8 kbps modem connection. The quality is rather good. There's something not quite right though. It does sound good, but you can tell that something has happened to it, like it's been recorded in a dustbin or something. This is particularly noticeable with real instruments, acoustic guitar, cymbals, that sort of thing.

I have a composer/musician friend who has used Quicktime to squash a 70MB audio file, of mainly electronic music, down to almost 1MB and it sounds great. This hints of great things to come in the realms of audio streaming, there is hope. It is also rumoured that this is going to be incorporated into the new MPEG 4 compression format for multimedia, cool.

As I finish that last paragraph RealNetworks email me to the effect that their latest version of RealAudio, entitled G2, is out and sounds better and faster than ever, which it does, a bit. I also read in the press that the next version G3 is being beta tested and will have arrived by the time this is published. There is no way of keeping track of all this. Suffice to say that the possibilities for music on the internet just get better and better.

## Copyright – yours

Publishing your music on a web page for free downloading is great. But what happens when you turn on the radio and hear someone else singing your song? Can you prove it's yours? Healthy paranoia can win court cases against major record companies. Before you publish your music, make a copy and put it in a jiffy bag. Include printed lyrics and sign and date everything. Seal the package and send it to yourself by registered post. *Don't* open it. Open it in court and the contents should be enough to prove you were the originator of the song. Better still take it to a bank and get them to lock it away, or send it to a solicitor. It could be worthwhile or it could be a load of fuss over nothing.

## Liquid Audio

One other possibility of note is Liquid Audio. This company is firmly on the side of the record companies and artists and distributes music over the internet on a pay-to-play basis. It's actually a very sound idea and utilises very advanced technology. Using the Liquid Audio Player you can preview tracks from albums in a streaming, low quality, format, then you can choose to buy that track. You splash out your plastic credit card and can download the track onto your hard drive in top CD quality. The Liquid Audio software also allows you burn the track onto a CD writer, if you have one, so you can make up your own compilation CD's safe in the knowledge that the artist has been paid. The player also shows sleeve notes and copyright information, it's all very above board.

This is quite a good opportunity for us struggling musicians and bands because by purchasing their compression software you can release your music on the net and receive royalties when people download them. They will put your tracks onto their main web pages so that anyone can browse on in and sample your music. This is the only way I'm aware of that secures royalty payments for your music over the internet.

The cheapest and easiest way to publish your music on the internet in my opinion is still MP3. All the software is free, the quality is great and it's all created by enthusiasts. RealAudio will get there but at the moment the possibilities are greater than what it actually delivers. Quicktime 3 is excellent, particularly for electronic music, but it's a high spec format so not everyone can run it, and the compression software costs money. If you're serious about your music and think you can play with the big boys then try out Liquid Audio, you never know what might happen.

## Check out my web page

I have assigned some web space on my companion web page to
show the latest in audio streaming and other goodies, as well as
links to all the stuff mentioned above.

Check my web page for the
latest

**http://www.pc-music.com**

# *Intermission* 10

hew! That's a load of information to take on board all at once. Crack open a beer, light a cigarette and take a moment to consider everything so far.

Do you know what you want to do yet?
Oh come on, what else do you need to know?

I hope, at least, that you now have some rudimentary understanding of what a PC can do for music. As I stated in the beginning, it all comes down to what you want to get out of this. Experiment and have fun, that's what this is all about. I could give you every example in the book, lead you step by step through the creative process, but it would be my creative process, yours may be vastly different. All these programs on offer give you the tools to create, it is up to you how you use them.

The products will all change and evolve over time as the stampede of technology cuts a swathe towards the future. Things which seem out of reach or impossible now will soon become simple programs. It's an exciting industry to be involved with and the tools on offer can add a whole new perspective to the creative process, or just simply let you have fun.

Music can be a gift, recording is much more of a skill. Give yourself time, try reading the manuals, and just try things out. Not everyone can be a star, I should know, I've been doing this stuff for 14 years and the most I ever made out of my music was 25 quid which was spent on a well deserved curry. I'll keep going at it though because it gives me pleasure and there's always that carrot of fame and fortune dangling tantalisingly just out of reach.

## Give it a go

The later chapters of this book deal with PC music in more practical terms – showing you how to handle Windows, suggesting ways of setting up your studio (term used very loosely), and lists of products and contacts to give you an idea of what's actually out there to buy.

# *Tackling Windows*

aving a basic grasp of the media functions within Windows 95/98 is pretty essential to the overall PC music making experience.

A PC with some form of soundcard (sometimes termed a 'Multimedia PC') contains all the basic ingredients for music making so we need to find out exactly what these are, where they came from, and how they relate to each other.

Assuming you have some sort of soundcard and a speaker device connected to the output, we'll dive into Windows and try to get some sound out of it.

When you turn your computer on and Windows boots up you may be greeted by a sort of washy tinkly sound. That sound is called 'The Microsoft Sound' and is a piece of audio being played back off your hard drive. If you heard nothing at all, don't panic, your PC may not be set up to play back sound on opening Windows. If you hear nothing from the next bit then you can start to panic.

### INFO

*T*he Microsoft Sound was allegedly created by Brian Eno

## Let's play something

Right, let's get Windows to play some sound. Open 'Media Player'. This can be found under the Start menu. Click on Start, go up to Programs, then Accessories, then Multimedia and you should find 'Media Player'. It will look something like Figure 11.1.

Click on 'File' and 'Open'. Hopefully it will open directly into the 'Media' directory, if not 'Media' can be found under the 'Windows' directory. If you still don't see any files click on the 'Files of Type' menu and select 'all files'.

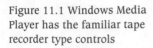

Figure 11.1 Windows Media Player has the familiar tape recorder type controls

You should now see a number of files of at least two types. One type will have an icon of a little loudspeaker on a sheet of paper (if you already bought a sequencer or audio recording editor then the icons may be associated with that program and, therefore, look different). 'The Microsoft Sound' should have one of these. This icon means that the file is an audio file – real sound recorded onto your hard drive. The other type will have an icon of a couple of musical notes on a sheet of paper and will probably have the title of a piece of classical music. This is a MIDI file and will play the synthesiser on your soundcard (if you're not sure what this all means, read the first few chapters again and stop jumping ahead!). For now let's hear some music.

Select 'The Microsoft Sound' and click 'OK'. Press the little 'play' button on the Media Player and you should hear the same sound that you heard when you first started Windows. How exciting!

Experiment with opening different audio files with the same icon, if there are any. Next select a MIDI file. Press 'play' and you should hear the plink plonk sound of your soundcard's synthesiser. It usually sounds pretty rubbish but then they probably threw in the soundcard free when you bought the PC.

If you are hearing nothing at all at this point it will one or more of four things.

1  You don't have a soundcard – hopefully we would have established this by now but do please see the earlier chapter on soundcards just in case.
2  You haven't connected your soundcard's output properly – check your wiring. Speaker out to speakers, or line out to line in on amplifier. Check the volume of your amp or speakers. If you're not sure which socket is the soundcard output then keep the Media Player playing and try your speakers in all of them.
3  The Windows volume controls are down – we'll come to this next.
4  Your soundcard isn't correctly set up within Windows – we'll tackle this after the volume bit.

# Volume control

This is staggeringly important and the cause of much unnecessary frustration and technical support. Windows has a volume control which controls the input and output (recording and playback) levels of your soundcard. The software that came with your soundcard may contain a flashy mixer, in which case use that and consult your documentation, but the concepts are the same as using the default Windows volume controls.

So where are they? Well, if you still have Media Player open then the Volume controls can be found under 'Devices'. Alternatively it can found under the Start menu in Multimedia the same as the Media Player. It should look something like Figure11.2 (the number of channels displayed will be dependent upon the capabilities of your soundcard and what channels have been selected to be shown).

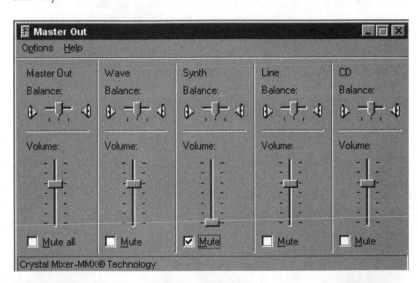

Figure 11.2 Volume controls

| Master out | Overall volume control of everything. |
| --- | --- |
| Wave | This is the audio volume control. Audio files are known as 'Wave' files because they have the extension '.wav' after them. |
| Synth | This is for the level of the soundcard's on-board synthesiser and so adjusts the volume of the MIDI playback. |
| Line | Overall level for line out. |
| CD | If you have a CD-ROM attached to your soundcard, this will adjust the volume of audio CDs. |

Now then, if you didn't hear anything when using the Media Player, check the relevant levels. In my volume control panel you can see that the synth channel is muted out and the level is at zero. If I tried to play back a MIDI file through my soundcard I would hear nothing at all. So in order to remedy this I need to deselect 'mute' and raise the level.

Click on 'options' and select 'properties'. This dialogue box allows you to make choice as to which volume controls you want to see and whether you want playback or recording controls.

## Recording controls

We'll take a quick look at the recording controls, so select them and press 'OK' (Figure 11.3).

These don't always make a huge amount of sense but there are two important ones, Line and Mic. By checking the box on a channel it allows your soundcard to record audio though that input. So, if you plugged a microphone into your soundcard you should select the Mic channel or you will be recording nothing. The grey box next to the volume slider will show the recording level in the form of coloured blocks (like LEDs), and you should adjust the slider in order to achieve the required recording level.

Let's have a quick go at recording something. Either, plug the microphone that came with your soundcard into the mic input, or, if you can play CDs through your soundcard, then stick in an audio CD.

Open up 'Sound Recorder' (Figure 11.4), also found under 'Multimedia'. Speak into the microphone, or play the CD and you

Figure 11.3 Recording controls

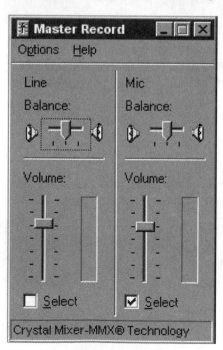

Figure 11.4 Sound Recorder

should see lines of green blobs appearing in the sound recorder window as above. If not then let's check the recording input. Open up the recording volume control again. If you are using a mic then select the mic input, if you are using a CD then select the line input. Give it another go. With any luck you'll be hard disk recording, if not, read on.

## *Sound management within Windows*

So how does Windows relate to your soundcard and other music making devices attached to your PC? To see what's going on you need to delve into the 'Control panel' (Figure 11.5). You can get to it either through the Start menu under Settings or by double-clicking the 'My Computer' icon.

There are two icons we are interested in here, Multimedia and System. Multimedia is where all the sound and music facilities

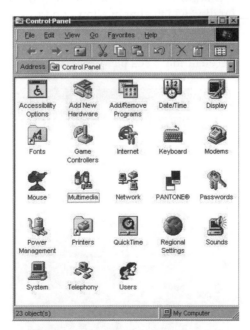

Figure 11.5 Control panel window

within windows are configured. System shows you where devices are installed and allows you to resolve any conflicts that arise when you install a new bit of hardware.

## Multimedia

Double-clicking the multimedia icon will bring up the display shown in Figure 11.6. The parts that we are interested in are Audio, MIDI and Devices (or 'Advanced' in Windows 95).

### Audio window

The 'Audio' window shows you your soundcard's configuration for recording and playback. The preferred device is where you can choose which soundcard will be doing the playback, and which will be recording. This is only useful if you have more than one soundcard. What is actually written there depends on your soundcard. In this example the name of the chipset on the soundcard is used to identify it, not very helpful but then fairly unimportant. You may find something more useful like 'Sound Blaster Out' for instance. It doesn't really matter as long as it somehow refers to your soundcard.

Ticking the 'show volume control on task bar' box will put a little speaker icon next to the clock on your task bar. This can be helpful because to get to Windows volume controls all you have to do is right click the icon and select 'open volume controls'.

The 'Advanced Properties' (Windows 98 only) button takes you to a window where you can specify things like 'sample rate conversion quality' which simply allows you to set whether you'd prefer to have better quality sound or better system performance. Set it to best quality, I'm sure your PC can cope with it. 'Hardware Acceleration'? Yes please.

Figure 11.6 Multimedia properties are listed here

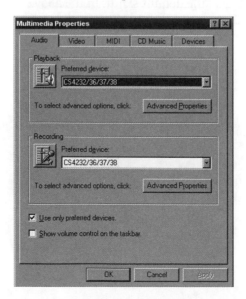

In Windows 95 on the recording part it allows you to choose preferred recording quality. Best to choose CD quality really as that's the best and we are trying to be a little bit professional here.

## MIDI window

The 'MIDI' window, shown in Figure 11.7, displays all the MIDI devices you have attached to your PC.

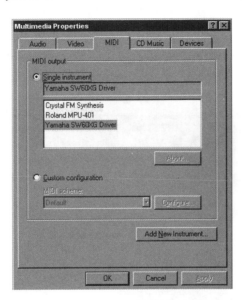

Figure 11.7 The MIDI window lists all the MIDI devices connected to your PC

A modern run-of-the-mill soundcard will usually have three MIDI devices:

### Wavetable synth
This is the main synth on a card and contains the best quality sounds. This is usually selected as the default synth. In the above example the Yamaha SW60XG (a stand alone hardware synth card) is acting as the wavetable synth because it has much better instrument sounds than my other soundcard synth which I have disabled.

### FM synth
This is an old school synth found on the first soundcards like the Sound Blaster V2. This was an impressive form of synthesis in its day and was the basis of professional synthesisers like Yamaha's legendary DX7. It sounds a bit poor nowadays but its presence is to ensure 'SoundBlaster Compatibility' so that the music in older games and other programs can still be played.

### MPU-401
A few years ago Roland invented a driver which enabled them to

use the joystick port of a soundcard as a MIDI interface. That driver
is called the Roland MPU-401 and lets you plug a MIDI keyboard
into your computer and start making music. Soundcard
manufacturers often use their own driver and call it an 'External
MIDI driver' or something similar.

To select a synth as the default simply click on it and press
'Apply'. If you were hearing nothing with the MIDI file playback
earlier then maybe you had an external device selected as default,
in which case the soundcard would remain silent while it pumped
the MIDI information out of its joystick port.

The 'Devices' window (or 'Advanced' in Windows 95) shown in
Figure 11.8 simply displays what media devices are attached to
your system. You can often access their system settings and disable
various bits if you fancy.

Figure 11.8 The 'Advanced'
window in Multimedia
Properties simply displays
what media devices are
attached to your system

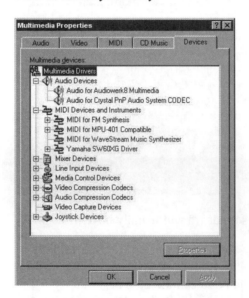

In the above example I have three different cards installed in my
PC giving me six different devices:

**Audiowerk8**
This is a professional audio-only card used with Emagic's Logic
Audio sequencer and hard-disk recording program. This card really
only works within Logic Audio but Emagic have produced a driver
to allow the card to be used by Windows as any other card with
limited functionality.

**Orchid NuSound**
This is a games/multimedia card which is pretty old but does the
job. It provides audio in and out with the Crystal PnP Audio System,
as well as Wavetable, FM and MPU401 MIDI devices.

**Yamaha SW60XG**
This is a synth-only card and provides a half decent set of MIDI instruments.

Your set-up may look very different but you should have at least one audio device and a couple of MIDI devices supplied by your soundcard.

# System

Finally we'll briefly look at the 'System' window just to see where soundcards are listed (Figure 11.9). You'll find the 'System' icon back in the 'Control Panel'.

Your soundcard devices can be found under 'Sound, video and game controllers' as in Figure 11.9. Some devices may not be listed, like the Yamaha SW60XG for instance. This is because it is not a Windows 95/98 native device. Many MIDI interfaces fall into this category and it is nothing to worry about. You just have to be aware that when choosing resources for a new device you also need to check in the Multimedia window for other devices not listed here. If you find that confusing then don't worry about it and pretend I never said anything because it's not essential.

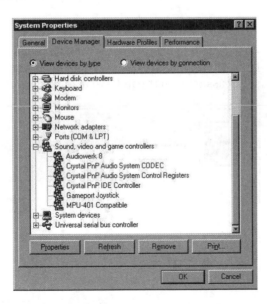

Figure 11.9 The System window

# 12 ★ PC music setups

## Your first studio

Well, here it is, your very first music production studio, impressive isn't it? Okay, let's explain what's going on by the numbers. This setup assumes that you have a soundcard in your PC.

Figure 12.1 A first music production studio

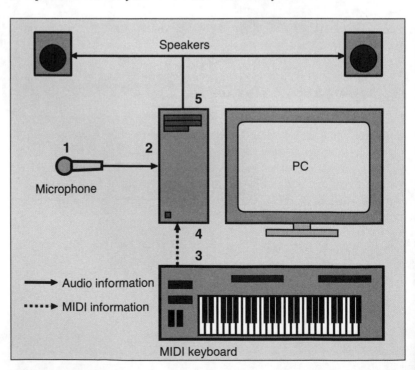

1  A microphone is used to record real sound – vocals, guitars, trombone, digeridoo etc.
2  The microphone is plugged into the 'Mic' socket on the soundcard so that the sound going through the microphone can be recorded.
3  The MIDI keyboard is a dummy keyboard. It has no sounds of its own, it's a controller keyboard being used to send MIDI note information to the PC.
4  The MIDI OUT of the keyboard is connected to the MIDI IN of the PC using an adapter cable attached to the soundcard's joystick port. The joystick port is providing the MIDI interface. This allows you to record the MIDI information generated by pressing notes on the keyboard and play it back through your soundcard's synth.
5  All the sound generated by the PC goes out of the soundcard's audio output. In this case the soundcard has a 'speaker' out, and so this is connected straight to the two speakers. The recorded audio plays back through this output. The MIDI synthesiser on the soundcard also plays its sounds through this output.

The only other thing you need is some kind of software which will allow you to record what you are doing. To do all the above you would need a combined hard disk recording and MIDI sequencer program. You also need a soundcard, a standard one should do with audio in and out and a joystick port for MIDI.

If you are not interested in recording real sound then all you need is the keyboard, interface and MIDI sequencing software. If you are not interested in MIDI then just the mic and hard disk recording software are required.

**INFO**

*C*ubase VST, Emagic Logic Audio and Cakewalk are some typical examples of combined hard disk recording and MIDI sequencer programs.

# The home project studio

You want to make some serious music, multitrack audio recording alongside MIDI using an external synthesiser. You're after good quality with the minimum of fuss.

The PC in this case contains an audio recording card with a stereo in and out, and a simple MIDI interface giving one MIDI IN and one MIDI OUT, this could be all on one card or on two separate ones.

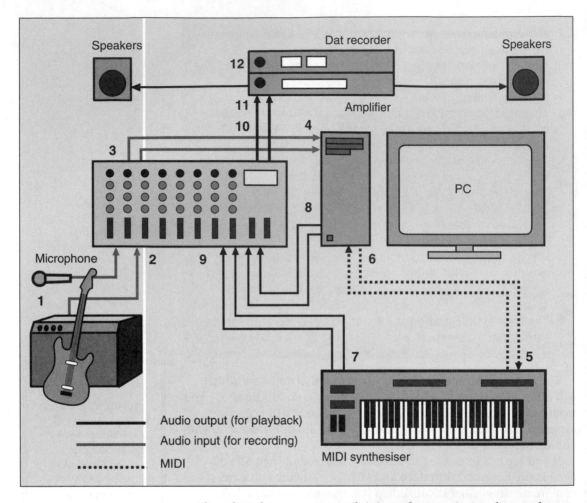

Figure 12.2 A home project studio

Okay, let's have a go at explaining what's going on by numbers.

1  You have a couple of sources to record. A microphone for vocals and a guitar. If the guitar amplifier has a direct output then you could record using that, otherwise you could mic up the amplifier.

2  Sound that's going to be recorded onto the PC (vocals through a microphone, the output of a guitar amp, whatever) should go into the mixer before going into the PC. Why? It's a great deal easier to plug your microphone into a mixer than it is fiddling about around the back of PC trying to plug a 1/4 inch jack into a pathetic mini-jack hole on a soundcard. If you are using a condenser mic then a mixer can provide phantom powering. It just makes life simpler.

3  This bit's a little tricky so concentrate. So, you want to record a vocal track. You'll also want to hear what you are

about to sing along to. Okay, vocal mic goes into the mixer, and so does the output of whatever accompaniment you are using (keyboard sequence, previously recorded audio tracks, etc.). If you plug the main output of the mixer into the soundcard then you will record everything going through the mixer onto a single track on the PC. That's no good (if you're still with me at this point then you'll agree). What to do? Couple of options here depending on your mixer.

(i)   If you have more than a 'mix' output on your mixer then route the mic to a different output. e.g. a separate 'bus' if you have a multi bus mixer, or 'monitor' output.

(ii)  Use an 'auxiliary'. These are used for routing channels to external sound processors, so pretend that your PC is a sound processor and take an auxiliary to the soundcard.

(iii) Use a direct out, if you have one, from the mic channel straight to the soundcard.

4  The input on a soundcard is invariably a stereo mini-jack socket, like that found on a walkman. These are a pain and more than a little unprofessional. This is where the mixer is handy again. It is far better to take a stereo out from the mixer to the soundcard using a properly made up cable, rather than plugging an instrument or mic straight in via an adapter. The mixer can also stay connected so you don't ruin an already poor socket by constantly plugging in and unplugging instruments.

5  The MIDI part of the set-up is represented by a MIDI keyboard synthesiser. The sound of the synthesiser is not actually recorded as audio but is 'controlled' by the MIDI sequencer on the PC. The MIDI OUT of the keyboard is connected to the MIDI IN of the PC so that MIDI information can be played and recorded onto the PC. The MIDI OUT of the PC is connected back to the synthesiser MIDI IN to use the synthesiser's sounds on playback.

6  The MIDI interface on the PC can be as simple as the joystick port on the soundcard, or can be anything up to eight MIDI INs and OUTs.

7  On playback, the MIDI sequence plays the sounds on the synthesiser, and so the output of the synthesiser should go to the mixer.

8  The output of the audio soundcard will contain all of the recorded audio tracks, and should be plugged into the mixer. It'll be a stereo signal so plug it into two channels on the mixer (using a stereo mini-jack to two 1/4 inch jack cable).

9  Everything you want to hear on recording and playback goes into the mixer.

10 The 'mix' output of the mixer goes to your amplifier so you
can hear it. If you don't have an amp then plug some
headphones into the headphone socket on the mixer and put
them on your head.

11 When your song is finished then 'mix down' to a DAT
recorder, or cassette, or CDR. 'Mix down' means press play
on the PC, set the levels on the mixer until you think it
sounds all right, press play and record on DAT machine,
press play on the PC again. Your finished song has just been
'mix downed' to DAT. The alternative of course is to mix
down back onto the PC. You could either record the output of
the synthesiser onto the PC as audio and mix down
internally, or plug the output of the mixer into the PC and
record the whole lot as one track. Finish off the recording in
a mastering program and burn to CD.

A good note to make here is about recording your MIDI sources onto
your PC as audio. If you are planning to mix everything on the PC
and then master to CD or whatever then you will need to record all
of the MIDI instrument tracks as audio. While they are still MIDI
tracks the actual sound is coming out of the MIDI device. You need
to record this sound onto the PC as you would an audio track. It's
easily done by 'soloing' the MIDI track you want to record and plug
the output of the MIDI device into your audio card input (or through
the mixer). You will then have a recording of what the MIDI device
played and can now mix down internally to a single stereo wave
file. Now you won't need the MIDI device any more so don't forget
to turn it off or down on playback or delete or mute its MIDI track.

The software used in this instance would probably be a combined
MIDI/audio recording package. Something with a good set of editing
features, support for plug-in effects and virtual mixing.

Phew! I hope that made some kind of sense. It all comes down to
what gear you have. Even if you're just recording from a single
rubbish mic then I would still advise getting hold of a simple mixer.
You may have an old 4-track portastudio knocking around, so use
that!

## A professional solution

This time the centre of our studio is the digital mixer. A digital
mixer, amongst other things, acts as the ADC, converting all
analogue inputs into digital audio which can then be routed directly
to the PC for recording. This PC has a digital interface card, a
common format would be ADAT optical, which offers eight tracks of
digital audio data down a single fibre optic cable. The PC also has a
couple of AV (audio/video) SCSI hard drives attached. These are very
fast and stable drives onto which the audio is recorded.

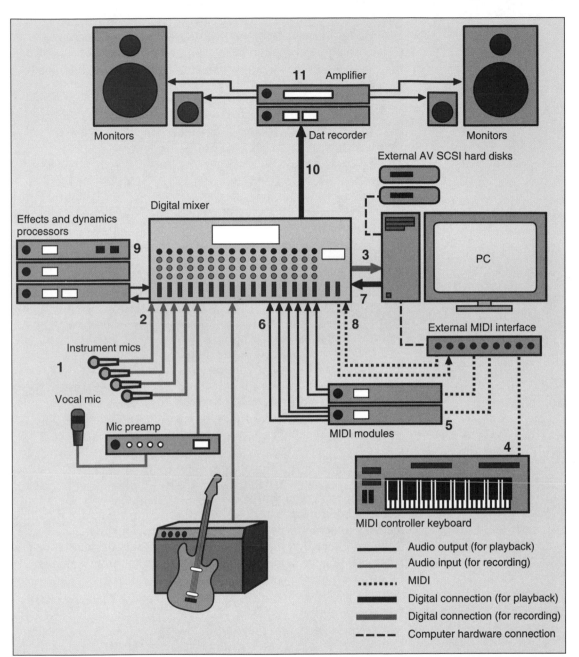

**11** Amplifier

Monitors

Dat recorder

Monitors

External AV SCSI hard disks

**10**

Digital mixer

Effects and dynamics processors

PC

**9**

**3**

**7**

**2**

**6**

**8**

External MIDI interface

Instrument mics

**1**

Vocal mic

Mic preamp

MIDI modules

**5**

**4**

MIDI controller keyboard

——— Audio output (for playback)
——— Audio input (for recording)
·········· MIDI
▬▬▬ Digital connection (for playback)
▬▬▬ Digital connection (for recording)
- - - - Computer hardware connection

Let's follow those numbers and try not to get lost.

Figure 12.3 A professional solution for recording multiple sources using a digital mixer

1 We now have multiple recording sources. Could be from a choir, brass section, or a drum kit which have to be recorded together. In this setup the PC can record anything up to eight separate tracks at a time, so multiple sources are not a problem. We also have a high quality condenser vocal microphone. This is put through a nice valve pre-amplifier which adds a warm sound to vocals before it's routed to the mixer.

2 All audio sources are put into the mixer through balanced inputs which help to cancel out any noise picked up by the cabling.

3 The audio sources are converted to digital audio by the mixer and routed directly into the PC via the ADAT optical interface for recording onto the hard disks.

4 The MIDI information is generated by our MIDI controller keyboard and sent to the PC through an external MIDI interface attached to the PC's parallel port.

5 This MIDI information is played back through some nice and expensive MIDI modules (or devices). One may be a high end synthesiser, another one a sampler.

6 The audio outputs of the MIDI devices are plugged into the mixer. MIDI modules can have many outputs, samplers commonly have eight to allow the individual instrument or sample sounds to utilise their own channel on a mixer.

7 The recorded audio is returned to the mixer on playback as eight separate tracks via the ADAT optical interface again.

8 Tricky new bit here concerning MIDI control or MIDI automation. The digital mixer has a MIDI IN and OUT. Each time a fader is moved MIDI controller information is generated which can also be recorded into the PC's sequencer. This means that on playback any fader movements would also be played back by the sequencer, on some mixers this means that the faders physically move in a most ghostly manor. Other elements of the mixer can also be allocated MIDI controllers and therefore controlled by the sequencer. So you no longer need 16 hands to mix a piece of music – cool.

9 Here comes another important reason for the use of a mixer – external effects and dynamics processing. Individual or groups of tracks can be routed through various boxes to change or enhance their sound. This may be compression, valve EQ, delays, reverbs, gates, enhancers, or a whole stack of other bits and pieces. I'll explain a bit more about why these are used at the end.

10 Direct digital out of the finished mix to DAT for mastering. Alternatively this could be routed back into the PC via a digital input and mastered on the computer.

11 Finally your music is returned to analogue audio by the DAT machine, sent through an amplifier and output to a quality pair, or selection, of studio monitors.

Using a digital mixer isn't actually that crucial to this setup. An analogue mixer would work in much the same way and also might be useful in adding warmth to your digital recording. Some people are more at home with the facilities and layout of an analogue mixer and find digital mixers far too annoying and complicated. The only difference it would make to our setup here is that you would need to add a multiple input/output ADC/DAC in order to convert the output of your analogue mixer into digital for the PC (and back again). These hardware converters are becoming more common and reasonably priced and so recording multiple simultaneous tracks onto your PC is within easy reach of the home studio user.

## External effects or plug-ins?

So, why use all these external effects when you have a whole bunch of software effect plug-ins? Well, a couple of reasons. Software plug-ins are fabulous but they tend to use a load of processing power. If you've got a 16 track song you may want to apply reverb to each one independently, chorus to a few others, compression on a couple more and a delay on some others. This is okay if you have a blistering hot PC, but for most of us the PC will fall over. You may not be able to apply all the effects you want. If you have an external effects processor you could put a thousand tracks through it and a load of other boxes and they wouldn't even break a sweat.

Another reason is that you may be more familiar with the way an external processor works or there's this one particular unit that you really like the sound of and always use. They are also have the advantage of being 'touchy-feely'.

### INFO

There isn't a plug-in for everything yet and there is tons of choice in quality, features and sound in the external processor market. They are just more real.

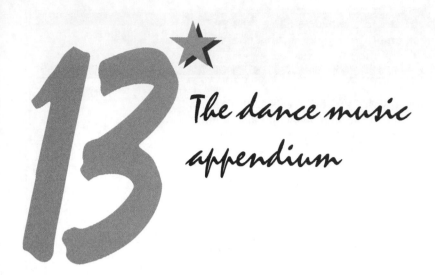

# 13 The dance music appendium

Computers and modern electronic dance music go hand in hand, they are inseparable and obvious bed fellows. In fact many people believe that this is the only use of computers in music. Hopefully I've shown you otherwise. In writing this book I have avoided being genre or style specific, simply because everything I have talked about is applicable to any sort of music, but I think it would be good to take a look at the sort of tools used on computer to generate dance, house, techno, trance, acid, jungle, drum 'n' bass, ambient or whatever it is you want to call it (I'll refer to it as 'dance' for simplicity).

The beauty of dance music is that it doesn't require any musical training or ability to play an instrument. Anyone can do it. The friendly user interface and robotic timing of the computer has brought 'banging beats' to the masses. The music isn't necessarily played into the computer but rather 'programmed' with the use of mouse. A favourite way of entering notes is using the piano-roll editor or, even better, the drum grid if your sequencer has one. You could look at a single bar, overlay a grid of 16 beats and put a closed hi-hat on every line. Follow that with a bass drum on every 4th, and an open hi-hat on the off beat (2nd, 6th, 10th and 14th) and you have a classic dance music drum pattern. If you find this a little uninspiring and really can't seem to come up with the pattern you're after then there are a range of drum pattern MIDI files available on disk. Simply open the file and copy-and-paste the patterns into your song. How easy is that? Mind you, if you're

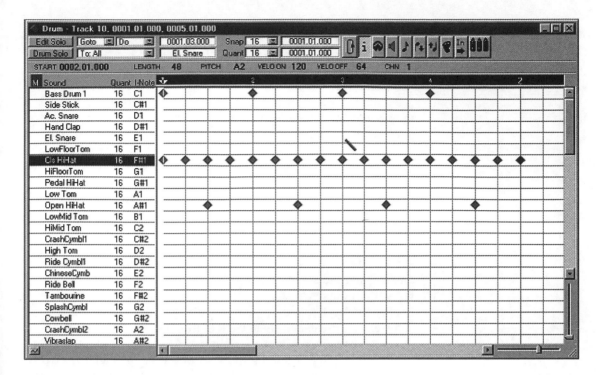

Figure 13.1 Steinberg's Cubase VST Drum Grid Editor

going to let someone else do all the music for you, you may as well pack it in and put on a CD! But it's a start and it may give you some ideas.

You can make dance music with anything. You could knock out some beats with a tin can and a stick if you like, but there are some common tools of the trade that no self respecting dance musician/programmer should be without.

# Sampler

Now I've talked about this earlier in the book so hopefully you'll understand that a PC cannot be used as a sampler without the help of additional hardware or a software sampler. Quick recap – a sampler is a device which holds a piece of audio which is triggered for playback via MIDI.

## Why do you need a sampler?

There are three main uses of samplers in dance music:

Drum sounds
Loops
Hits

The drum sounds on your soundcard probably sound a bit flat and tinny. With a sampler you can copy a drum sound and use it in your own music, or you can buy a 'Sample CD' which has drum sounds already sampled for you. The exact same thing can be done with loops and hits.

A loop is a short piece of music, often percussion or an instrument riff, which is of a precise length so that when the playback is looped back to the beginning the sampled music is seamlessly repeated in time with itself. A hit is like a small musical event – a stab of a brass section or orchestra, a cymbal crash, vocal shout, or something of the like.

So, rather than programming your own patterns and phrases you can simply trigger loops and hits from your sequencer. People have been doing a similar sort of thing with twin record decks for years.

The computer can make another useful appearance here as a sample editor. Hardware samplers can be connected to a PC via SCSI and transfer the samples across for editing. This can also be done via MIDI but takes a very long time. You can then use software like Sonic Foundry's Sound Forge or Steinberg's Wavelab to edit the samples and then send them back to the sampler. Editing may include the removal of noise, trimming the sample so it's the right length for looping, trimming the start of the sample, adding effects or just generally mucking about with them.

A terribly useful piece of software is Steinberg's Recycle. It does the relatively simple job of cutting up a loop into its component parts and arranging the now individual samples across a keyboard like a drum kit. Anyone who's tried doing this in a hardware sampler will tell you that it can take hours to do it by hand.

Figure 13.2 Akai S5000 Sampler

## So what about a software sampler?

This is becoming a more and more valid option. With a fast PC the power of software like Nemesys Gigasampler and Bitheadz Unity DS-1 can match the facilities of a hardware sampler and do a lot of other stuff their hardware colleagues cannot. No more messing around with SCSI or external boxes. You have all the editing and the sequencing on the same machine, masses of hard disk space to store samples and all for a few hundred quid less than a hardware sampler. Do be aware that a software sampler requires a whole stack of processing power to run successfully. Don't expect to have loads of audio tracks running along side. The advantage of hardware samplers lies in their quality construction and converters, real-time effects and filters, and multiple outputs so that you can mix each sound independently through an external mixer. That said, Gigasampler supports the Aark 20/20 8x8 in/out audio card from Aardvark so outputs are not a problem, and Unity DS-1 does have some real-time filters so they are definitely getting there.

## Filters

One of the more obvious tools is the filter, well, obvious once you know what it is. You would have heard the effect a hundred times usually on a synth bass sound, often applied to drums, sometimes used on anything and everything. To describe the effect of a filter in words is very difficult (I've been trying to do this for hours) and the best I can come up with is to say it makes a kind of a sweeping 'psshhhoowaaaaarrrh' sound. Hmmm, perhaps it's better to describe what a filter actually does and then you might be able to spot the effect yourself.

Essentially a filter acts as an imaginary gate through which user specified frequencies are blocked or allowed through.

There are many types of filters including 6 pole, 4 pole, 2 pole, resonant, hi-pass, band-pass, low-pass, comb, to name a few. EQ or equalisation is also a form of filtering. A filter does as the name suggests, it removes, or 'filters' a specified frequency range of an audio signal. A very common one is the low-pass filter. This allows (or passes) low frequencies through unchanged up to a specified frequency. All frequencies above this 'cut-off' point are blocked. So,

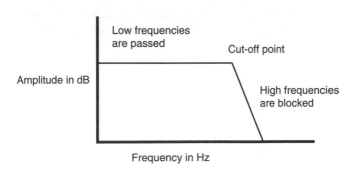

Figure 13.3 A simple low-pass filter blocks frequencies above the cut-off point

if you slowly increase the cut-off from zero to fully open you'll hear the gradual inclusion of higher frequencies in the sound giving a tonal raising in pitch effect.

Resonant filters are what we are more interested in as they have

Figure 13.4 A resonant filter
boosts frequencies at the
cut-off point

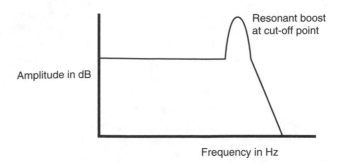

a special quality of boosting the frequencies at the cut-off point.
The amount of boost given to frequencies at this point and the
bandwidth is called 'resonance'. The 'cut-off' and 'resonance'
controls are two of the most overused in dance music.

Filters can't really be purchased by themselves, well there's the
odd one like the Waldorf 4 Pole or the Sherman Filter Bank, but
they are more often a feature of another piece of gear, like a
sampler or synth. Filtering plug-ins are available so that you could
apply it to an audio track in your hard disk recording software. For
an instant idea of what this all sounds like download Steinberg's
Rebirth demo and you'll find a resonance and cut-off knob on both
the MC303's.

## Analogue synths

Filters were utilised to full effect in analogue synthesis and the
sounds have lent themselves to dance music. Fat bass lines,
squelchy sounds, ethereal pads, and pure sounding leads come from
the guts of analogue synths. The sounds are dirty, raw, warm and
very broad in terms of dynamics and frequency, they just sound
great.

The biggest problem is that external analogue synths (or digital
'virtual' analogue synths, which aren't bad) are quite expensive. Or,
if you can find the original old style synths, they are often in bad
repair and rubbish at keeping in tune. The easiest solution for us
computer musicians is to get a software synth. The majority of
these are angled towards recreating analogue sounds and all the
ones I've tried sound pretty good. For around £100 – £200 you can
get something like Bitheadz Retro AS-1 and have fully multi-timbral
analogue synth on your PC – fantastic!!

## Sequencer

This would be a good idea. The standard has been Cubase for many
years for its ease of use and drum grid editor, but you can do the
same stuff with Logic, or Cakewalk, or any other sequencer.

# The Rest

There are loads of bits of software out there which will help you create dance music. Lots of them are simple sample based programs or instant 'techno' machines like Rebirth. These can be a lot of fun but if you want to start creating your own stuff then it's worth looking into sampling more than anything else. There are ways around buying a sampler, you can do a lot of sample based work in your hard disk recording/sequencer program. You can import a loop and copy-and-paste along the timeline. You can cut it up and create patterns by pasting the different parts of the loop on the arrange page. You can easily add hits by simply pasting them where you want them. This is all very time consuming though and can take a lot of fiddling to get it right. A good program for dealing purely with samples and loops is Sonic Foundry's ACID where you literally paint loops onto the screen and it time stretches the loops to keep them in time with each other.

Dance music – it's fun, it's easy, it's loopy and like all other styles of music, you can create absolute rubbish, but in a much shorter time. Don't forget that a sprinkling of talent can go a long way.

**TIP**

The only other requirement for making electronic dance music, of any form, is imagination and maybe a bit of drug taking, but that's just a stereotype, don't fall for it.

Figure 13.5 Sonic Foundry's ACID

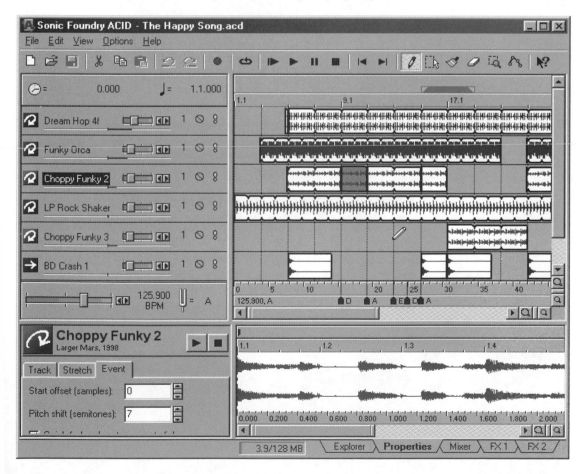

# 14 *The guitarist's appendium*

Guitarists are simple folk (I should know I am one), they know what they want and they don't like too much fuss. They just want to record their guitar, maybe some bass and a bit of drums, maybe even a vocal line. The most important thing they want is good quality, a broad dynamic sound, clear and precise, is that too much to ask? Not at all; let's look at some of the tools which will help the guitarists among you achieve the sound you're after.

## Getting the guitar into the computer

A soundcard is the first thing to look at. Usually soundcards have a microphone and a line input. Neither of these is particularly good for plugging an electric guitar straight in, the sound you'll get will be very thin and unexciting. I'd suggest that there needs to be a stage before the soundcard if you want to get a decent recorded sound. We've looked at this already in Chapter 12, but there are some more specifics that are worth going into. Essentially there are two options:

Pre-amp
Mic up the guitar amplifier

## Pre-amp

This is an increasingly interesting option. A pre-amp is a little amplifier in a box which raises the impedance of the guitar signal up to a that of a line signal. This done, the output can be plugged directly into the Line-in on the soundcard and you'll get a much better recorded sound. Pre-amps come in several shapes and sizes and you may not be aware that you probably already have one. A digital effects box contains a pre-amp and this is an ideal way of getting line level into your soundcard. So plug your guitar into your effects box before the computer. You don't have to use any effects if you don't want to, it's purely providing an input stage.

There are a couple of products that are designed purely to act as a pre-amp for a computer. Rocktron's PC Pre-amp is one such device and contains a clean and dirty channel with their patented 'Hush' noise reduction. It's even in that nasty PC buff colour so it'll match your whole set-up – nice!

Figure 14.1 Rocktron's PC Pre-amp – colour co-ordinated too

A much more dazzling one is the POD from Line6. The Line6 range of amplifiers contains a computer model of a number of classic amps which you can dial up depending on the type of sound you want. You want a 1960's Vox AC30 amp – no problem. They also contain effects all running at 24bit. The POD is simply the guts of the amp version without the speaker cone. In fact all their amps have a direct out which can be plugged straight into the computer. To top it all they have now released a software plug-in version which will give you all these amp models, including the original controls, on your screen. Currently it's only available for Digidesign Pro Tools TDM format, but it rocks!

Figure 14.2 Line6 POD – classic amp sounds on tap

### Mic up the amplifier

An easy, if noisy, option for most people. The best option if you want to capture the sound of your guitar/amp combination. The only problem is that you're introducing another 'quality' issue into your recording chain. Don't skimp on your choice of microphone. Paying a bit more for a good one will pay off in recording quality. Again it's worth going through a mixer or pre-amp before the soundcard.

## Adding external effects after recording

You've recorded a nice clean signal and now you want to add some effects to it. The plug-in effects you have might not cut it and you want to use your own effects boxes. This is easy if you have a multiple output soundcard as you could route the guitar track out of a single output to your effects box and record it back in as a separate track. If you have just a stereo in/out then the only way is to 'solo' the guitar track and put the output into your effects box. Listen to the effect until you're happy with it and then plug the output into the soundcard and record it as a separate track. It's not easy or ideal but you do get the required result.

## MIDI guitar synthesisers

Being a guitarist you don't necessarily play keyboards and you fancy putting some strings and synth sounds onto your songs. A good guitar synth can enable you to do this and there are MIDI pick-ups available from both Roland and Yamaha which will do a fine job. Remember, if you are using a MIDI guitar you are recording MIDI information through a MIDI interface and not actually recording the guitar sound. The sounds will come from whatever MIDI sound source you are using. Don't fall into the trap of recording guitar tracks as MIDI and wondering why the playback sound is a bit rubbish. If you want to record a guitar sound then record your actual guitar through a pre-amp or microphone.

## Software

Any hard disk recording program will do what you need it to. There is only one I know of angled at the guitarist which is Twelve Tone's 'Cakewalk Guitar Studio'. It's exactly the same as their 'Cakewalk Professional' package but uses a fret board diagram in place of the piano roll editor – may be useful. There are also loads of guitar tuition type programs around and those which generate an automatic backing group if you just fancy having a jam.

# Summary

Replacing your 4 track cassette machine with a computer and some hard disk recording software will give you power and possibilities you only dreamed of. I recommend strongly that once you've recorded your song you should muck around with it on screen in the arrange page. Copy and paste things around, chop things up, reverse things, and soon you'll find yourself in the exciting world of post production. It's not always rock and roll, but we like it.

## Contacts

Rocktron   (Soho Soundhouse Ltd) 0171 379 5148 (http://www.rocktron.com)
Line6      (Sound Technology) 01462 480000 (http://www.lin6.com)

# 15 Frequently asked questions

## What's best, Apple Mac or PC?

The Apple Mac is the most stable, fast, secure and easy-to-use computer. There, I've said it. Although this does depend on what you want the computer to be best at. There are many pros and cons of both formats and you have to weigh up the things that are important to you before making your choice.

Apple Macintosh computers are designed and constructed by one company. This makes them very stable and they require little setting up. The first Mac G3 computers were very powerful and handled music software extremely well. The latest G3 and the iMac's are a slightly different kettle of fish. Apple have made a brave step into the future by using the new USB (Universal Serial Bus) interface. Unfortunately most high end music software uses some kind of copyright protection which involves either a hardware 'dongle' which attaches to a normal serial port, or a 'key' floppy disk – iMac doesn't have a floppy disk drive. Also, at the time of writing, there are no USB MIDI or audio interfaces. These will be available by the time you read this but make sure you check out what's available before investing in an iMac or a new G3 for music.

IBM PC compatibles are made from bits and pieces from all over the place. Different manufacturers, different standards, incompatibility problems. This is why they tend to crash more often. Windows does a grand job of keeping it all together but sometimes there's just too much going on.

With a Mac, generally speaking, you can plug in some hardware, install some software, turn on the machine and it all works. With a PC you can plug in some hardware and hope Windows 95 picks it up and then fiddle around with its resource settings so that it fits around all the other bits you have in your computer. Install some software and hope that the hardware can communicate with it. It's not always like this and many things install with no problems at all, and Windows 98 goes a long way to sorting this all out much better than '95.

One massive difference between the two can be seen in the range of products available. The best music recording software/hardware was until recently Mac only – Digidesign's Pro Tools 24 – now available for Windows NT. After that there are maybe a half dozen other pieces of music software available for it. Hardware wise, after Pro Tools, there's a couple of audio PCI cards available. On the PC there are hundreds of pieces of music related software, dozens of different types of soundcards and audio cards, the choice is staggering. Companies who used to developed software purely for the Mac now release products first on the PC and follow up with the Mac version later.

The last consideration is price. Apple Macs are usually half as expensive again as a comparable PC. The software and hardware available for the Mac is similarly expensive. You can't do anything cheaply or low end on a Mac.

You have to choose for yourself. Having experience of both platforms I look at it this way: If you want a computer to run a single application, do a precise job with the minimum of fuss, and you can afford it, buy an Apple Mac. If you want a computer which is capable of producing the same results and is openly expandable, will run all sorts of other software and hardware, offers choice at an affordable level, and is supported by far more manufacturers, then I'd suggest you buy a PC. You'll just have to accept that a PC can be a bit flaky sometimes.

**IRONY**

*A*ll this mucking around with resources, memory and IRQs is, to me, why PCs are so much better than Macs. The PC has such an open architecture that allows you to plug in all sorts of odd bits and pieces, change it around, govern how things are connected, the user is really in charge and can tailor a system to his or her own requirements. With a Mac you turn it on and it works – where's the fun in that?

## What sort of specification do I need to look for in buying a PC?

With the relentless trudging forward of technology and processing power you will find that most PC music software requires Windows 95 running on a Pentium processor (or equivalent) and getting on for 32MB of RAM. Windows NT may be the operating system of the future but for now only a few products run under it. Besides if you're running NT you obviously know what you're doing, so I won't be any help (yeah right!).

### Simple answer
The biggest, shiniest, fastest, funkiest machine you can get your hands on.

*Long and involved answer*

Depends on what you're doing. For MIDI stuff, sequencing and notation, you don't need much at all. A 486 processor, if they still existed, would be fine. The problem is that everything is written for Windows 95, and that needs a Pentium with 16MB of RAM to run comfortably. So, any entry level Pentium based PC would do the job.

For audio stuff it's a different story. Handling and processing audio files, particularly in real-time, is processor-hungry stuff. Aim as high as you can, the faster your system the more you'll get out of a program. A Pentium running at 200MHz with 32MB RAM should be able to record up to 12 tracks of audio. If you want to add real-time effects then that number may drop down to eight. The type of audio interface you are using can make a big difference. For instance, a Pentium 166MHz with a standard soundcard will do about eight tracks of audio in Cubase VST, if instead of the soundcard you use an audio interface like the Lexicon Studio you will be able to do 24 tracks. You can of course run the software on a lower specification than I suggest, see how it goes and upgrade if necessary.

My recommendation for a glitch free and powerful recording PC would be a Pentium II 400MHz with 128MB RAM. A separate hard drive for audio would be handy, so would a large monitor.

### Is there anything special I should look for when buying a PC?

The first thing to consider when buying a PC is: what do you want it to do? If music creation and production is a priority then I would recommend the following: Purchase the most powerful, yet standard, machine you can lay your hands on. By 'standard' I mean:

- A case size that allows for easy access to the guts of the PC and is big enough to take a full length ISA or PCI card. If you can, check that the CPU is not situated behind the slots restricting the length of card you can put in.
- Has plenty of available ISA and PCI slots for upgrading.
- Has lots of room for extra drives, backup devices, CD writers etc.
- Does not have a soundcard or modem built onto the motherboard or onto each other. These are a complete pain to remove or disable when you want to slot in a better soundcard.
- Be careful about the type of video card. The newer AGP (Advanced Graphics Port) cards are the best option, otherwise contact the manufacturer of the music software you intend to use for a list of recommended video cards. Some can cause all sorts of problems with audio recording.

> Often the most simple cards are the best.
> - Avoid being given a load of pre-installed software which may be nice but will be taking up tons of hard disk space.
> - Make sure you are given the original disks for all the installed software. There are times when reformatting your hard drive and installing Windows from scratch is the only option.

PC's are designed and sold for business and entertainment. Don't expect a computer shop to know the first thing about music.

On the choice of CPU, Intel seem to be the best. Cyrix chips don't have very good floating point performance which is something that audio recording relies on. AMD are a good alternative to Intel and seem to perform well. Forget the new cheap range from Intel, it's for business machines only.

If you're a patient person and a little technical or logically minded, or just fancy a challenge, then I would recommend putting the PC together yourself. Get advice from computer parts suppliers, buy all the bits and get stuck in. You will learn so much about your computer that future upgrades and sorting our problems becomes a doddle. Of course you might end up throwing it out of the window in disgust.

To summarise, get yourself a simple, no frills system that is easily upgradable and, if possible, has an inbuilt ashtray.

## I already have a PC, how do I set it up for music?

Music programs involving audio will use every ounce of strength your computer can muster. So, you need to free up as much memory and resources as possible. Common memory eating culprits are things like:

### Automatic virus checkers.
Why on earth would your computer suddenly get a virus since the last time you turned it on? They don't magically appear, they have to be physically put on your system, even if inadvertently. If you're about to use a dodgy disk from somewhere then by all means run a virus checker on it, but there is no reason to have one on start-up or sitting around in the background.

### Screensavers
All very pretty and amusing ... for the first two seconds, but have you ever heard of anyone ever suffering from monitor burn through? Imagine that you've got a piece of music you've been working on and it's good, I mean really good, and you pause for a cigarette. Suddenly your screensaver cuts in and the computer can't really handle the added load and crashes badly. Screensavers are not worth it.

### Office software

No I don't mean that you should get rid of it. Many office products insist on launching on start-up and then sit in the background offering you a handy toolbar. Close it all down before using your music software.

### Active desktop

There is some argument over this but as far as I can see an active desktop uses up more system resources than the traditional Windows 95 desktop alone.

Anything else that starts up automatically when you boot Windows should be turned off or disabled.

If you hope to record audio then it's helpful (but not essential) to either have a separate hard drive for the audio or partition your existing one. Your hard drive will run more efficiently if the audio can be streamed off the same part of the drive. It also makes managing your work much easier.

Some kind of back-up device will become more important as you fill up your hard drive. I would suggest getting one straight away and back-up your whole Windows system before installing your music software and hardware, just in case it all goes horribly wrong. This is all good sense anyway. I lost my system hard drive recently, it just died, no warning, no smoke, just decided it had had enough. Luckily my music was all recorded on a separate drive, but I lost four years' worth of files and software that I had 'acquired' over that time and had to start with a fresh install of Windows 95 on a new hard disk. That experience impressed upon me the importance of backing up my work.

## But don't I need a special hard disk?

Lot's of people say that you have to be using a SCSI (small computer serial interface) AV (audio/video) hard drive to record audio. That is absolute nonsense maliciously put about by Apple Mac users and professionals who don't think normal people should have access to all this wondrous technology.

A fast SCSI AV drive is the ideal, but you only really need it if you are doing seriously large recordings, massive amounts of tracks, or need something which is going to be 100% reliable at all times, and time is money.

The reason is something to do with thermal calibration. A hard drive has to look at itself to make sure it's still doing what it should, and not catching fire or anything. So every ten minutes or so a hard drive glances at itself just to make sure. You may have noticed your drive light flickering from time to time for no apparent reason – it's recalibrating. Now, if it does this in the middle of a massive mix-down then there is the possibility that you'll get a drop-out or the drive will just fall over – not good. An AV drive is designed not to do this, and for this facility you have to pay staggering sums of money (they are also very fast which is a bonus). A standard EIDE drive will be plenty for most of us, if you have problems then sort it out and buy a SCSI card and an AV drive, but in the meantime get on with what you have.

## How much hard disk space does recording take up?

MIDI recording takes up bugger all. Audio recording eats hard drives for breakfast. The rule of thumb is: 5MB per minute per track. So, an eight track song will use 40MB per minute, three minute song, 120MB. This assumes that you are recording at CD quality (16bit 44.1kHz). Lowering the sample rate or resolution reduces the recording time by the same factor. If you copy and paste something then it will only use up the disk space of the original, and if you delete any silent areas you'll never use as much as you think.

## What about Windows 98 or NT 5?

There has been a lot of discussion about this in the industry and the press, most of it pretty boring. My feeling is that if your system is running fine under Windows 95 then don't mess with it. If you want to jump onto the Windows 98 bandwagon then I would strongly recommend only doing it as a clean install. I have heard of people having strange problems when upgrading over the top of Windows 95, it can be unstable, all the usual first edition problems. At the end of the day Windows 98 should make for a better, cleaner and more efficient system, just use a touch of caution.

NT 5 is where everything will have to go. At the moment NT seems to have trouble dealing with MIDI and audio and there are only a few products that will run under it. I'm sure when version 5 does arrive it will all be hunky-dory.

With future updates like the proposed Windows 2000, your best course of action is to contact the manufacturer of your music hardware/software before upgrading, just to check stability and whether they will support you using that system.

One more interesting operating system is the new BeOS which is a cross platform operating system based upon Java and other internet languages and protocols. Many music software companies, including Steinberg and Emagic, have pledged support for this sharing, caring funky and fast operating system. Certainly one to keep an eye on.

## What do I need to get professional results?

This is an interesting an complicated question. The definition of 'professional' seems to be constantly changing, is often confusing, and is rather dependent on your own point of view.

In music recording, 'professional' tends to mean quality, reliability, big pieces of hardware, and a hefty price tag (professionals also seem to carry shoulder bags. How this fits into the definition has yet to be fully explained). Over time the goal posts are pushed further and further away so that something used for 'professional' recording ten or even five years ago, is now considered obsolete.

To me, professionalism is a combination of the gear you are using and the skills with which you use it. There is no reason why you can't get professional results using a simple tape based four track machine, or even just a tape recorder and a microphone. If you know what you're doing then the gear becomes less and less important. Obviously a lot of people would say that I am talking complete rubbish and being professional requires years of training and stacks of really expensive studio gear, and of course a shoulder bag. I could respond by using the 'Beatles White album was recorded on a clapped out old four track' cliche and also point out that it's often the limitations of your set-up that produce the most interesting experimentation and strokes of genius. This is all a pointless argument because everyone's perceptions are different.

The best way to perceive professionalism is not in terms of the finished product but in the terms of the way you work and your working environment. The industry will tell us that we are essentially talking about the quality of the tools you use. Let's take a relevant example – a soundcard for audio recording.

Your standard soundcard can record audio onto your hard drive. The quality is okay for your purposes, it's a little noisy in places, but acceptable. Your microphone input is a mini-jack connector so you have a jack-to-minijack adapter on the end of your mic cable. It all works, why would you need anything else?

The 'professional' solution would be a little different. The soundcard would be dedicated to audio recording. The card itself would act purely as an interface to the computer. The actual conversion of the analogue signal into digital information would take place in an external unit, this way there is no problem of picking up noise from inside the PC. The connection into the unit would be a balanced XLR connector, which the microphone can plug straight into. The unit could also provide phantom powering for the higher quality condenser microphones. The unit has on board DSP (digital signal processors) which remove all the audio processing away from the PC's CPU, making the software run more efficiently. The result is, a faster system, a cleaner signal, less physical wear on your hardware, the possibility of more tracks and more effects within the software.

The difference in price between these two systems could amount to thousands of pounds. Is it worth the difference? Yes, because you get a system which gets the most out of the software you are using, makes your life easier, and you get a nice new box with flashing lights on it. The point is that you get a system which works, and works to the full. Having this expensive gear won't make you a professional, but the better you gear is, the easier it will be to adopt a professional attitude to what you are doing.

People demand increasingly professional products for less and less money. The power now available to the average punter is staggering, but to make the fullest use of this power will cost money. If you want the best you have to pay for it, there is no way out of it.

Okay, you can buy a three hundred pound piece of software, like Emagic's Logic, and a five hundred pound soundcard and get some stunning results. Plug that piece of software into Digidesign's Pro Tools costing around ten thousand pounds, and you will hear and see a difference. You will see the program running how it always should have. No delays, no stutters, no falling over at odd moments, instant playback, accurate monitoring, all the tracks all at once with all the effects and EQ. To make this happen you need the right hardware and a cheap soundcard could not really be considered to be the right hardware. That said, if you know what you are doing then you can produce magical stuff with very little. Conversely you could have all the gear money can buy and still not produce anything worth listening to.

A useful analogy would be if you went out and bought some really expensive paint and a perfect, hand-crafted paint brush, you could still make a complete pig's ear out of painting your house.

Just remember, when your PC crashes, when you run out of tracks, when you can't get things to synchronise properly, sit back and look at the fabulous power you have at your fingertips. Remember the complete lack of editing facilities on your 4 track porta-studio, the hiss of tape, the wow and flutter, the expense of it all, and consider yourself fortunate to be given such incredible tools. Have a professional attitude to your music and get the best out of what you have.

## How do I put my finished music onto an audio CD?

Get yourself a CD writer. Actually it's not always that easy. The simplest way is to buy an external stand-alone CD-R (Compact Disc Recorder) which acts just like a hi-fi cassette recorder. You literally plug the audio output of your computer into the CD-R and press record. They also have digital inputs so you could transfer your music digitally, either from your computer if you have a digital output, or from a DAT machine if you have already mastered to that.

Most people, however, want a CD-R which is built into their computer so they can back-up software and stuff as well. This is where you need to be a little careful. CD-Rs are built by computer manufacturers for storing computer data. The ability to record audio CDs is a bonus. As they weren't originally designed for this purpose many CD-Rs don't cope with audio recording very well if at all. There are certain standards required in the manufacturing of audio CDs so that the resultant CD can be played back in a normal domestic CD player. The digital audio has to be streamed onto the CD at a steady rate. Computer data can be splattered all over the CD, constant streaming is not important. The digital audio has to be encoded with P&Q information, which is essentially defined start and stop points and pauses between tracks. Other non-essential things like track listings are also useful. This is referred to as the Red Book Standard, and is the standard by which audio CDs are made. There are other standards, most familiar will be Orange Book which refers to how multimedia CDs are made, and it's this standard, not Red Book, that the majority of CD-Rs, and their accompanying software, are designed to support.

However, after saying all that, the main thing that determines whether you can create an audio CD is the writing software you use. The process of creating an audio CD is called Red Book Mastering, so you need a piece of software that can do that. Steinberg's Wavelab is one such piece of software. It's a full on audio editing program which includes the ability to encode your finished audio for red book mastering to CD. There are a few others and simple ones are often included with a CD-R drive.

### So which CD-R should I get?

The best way to ensure success is to consult the manufacturers of Red Book mastering software about which CD-R drives they support. My advice would be as follows:

- Don't buy the cheapest you can find. Unlikely to do audio very well.
- Go for SCSI over EIDE. SCSI tends to be faster and so better at keeping up a constant stream. In making a CD the audio is transferred from your hard drive onto the CD, having an EIDE CD-R along side your EIDE hard drive means that the computer has to keep switching between devices on the same bus. Operating two busses simultaneously is much more efficient.
- Get an external drive rather than an internal drive. All the devices within your PC are driven by a single power supply. You probably already have a couple of hard drives, a floppy drive and a CD-ROM running off it. If, while burning a CD you get a small power fluctuation, the power supply may be too stretched to compensate and subsequently ruin your disk. It'll only do this, of course, when you hit 95% of completion. It sounds a little odd I know, but this has happened to me a number of times and the only solution was

to put the CD-R in an external case with its own power supply.
• Get some good Red Book mastering software.

## What about re-writable CDs?

CD-RW or re-writable CDs are a superficially great idea. However, re-writable CDs cannot be played on normal CD players, so they are pointless for mastering audio CDs. Also the price of re-writable media is about ten times that of a normal recordable CD. So, why spend the time deleting a re-writable CD (takes as long as it did to record the thing) when you could use another normal recordable CD at the tenth of the price. It doesn't matter if you have a re-writable drive or not, you'll hardly use the re-writable function.

## I've heard that digital recordings lack 'warmth': what's that all about?

Digital recordings have often been accused of sounding somehow too clean or clinical when compared to a recording made on an analogue system. This is a different issue to that of quality. Digital systems record audio much more accurately than their analogue counterparts, but this is not always what we are happier listening to. Any piece of electrical analogue equipment adds to the sound going through it. This is often called 'colouring'. Recording to an analogue tape based system the recording tends to lose some of the top end, the higher frequencies. Repeat the recording onto a hard disk digital system and everything would be faithfully reproduced, including the high frequencies. The difference to the listener would be that the analogue recording would sound less harsh, or 'warmer' than the digital version.

Is this making any sense yet? It's a very subjective thing and so quite hard to explain. It's like people who prefer the sound of vinyl over CD. Analogue recordings have a 'sound' of their own and are generally considered to be warmer and more pleasing to the ear.

So, what do you do about this on your nice new PC digital recording system? There are ways that you can reintroduce warmth back into your recordings, and this is the reason why you will find so much revamped old technology knocking around. Valves seem to be the key. Valves in amplifiers were done away with a number of years ago in favour of the cheaper and more rugged transistor circuits. They still hung on in guitar amplifiers because of the warm sound they produced. The warmth of valves elsewhere was only really missed when studios turned to digital audio. Suddenly everything sounded too clean, too nice, too perfect, and this didn't suit every kind of music. So, people rescued their old valve pre-amplifiers from the dustbin and started using them again. Now you'll find loads of new products containing valve technology. All of them designed to re-introduce the nice warm and dirty sounds that we love so much.

It's good to see that some areas of the music industry are still governed by what we like to listen to rather than the latest advances in technology.

### Is there any software which will convert my voice or another instrument into MIDI?

Converting audio into MIDI is hard, really hard, I mean it's a very awfully difficult thing to do, and although it can be done, let's face it, it's rubbish. The conditions needed to make this work well are as follows:

1 Has to be a monophonic source. This means one note at a time, no chords, only a single instrument playing a single note at a time.
2 The source has to contain a very strong fundamental tone. This means that the sound should be very pure, no or few harmonics. Flute is a good example.
3 Has to be a clear separation between the notes. Legato notes are no good.

To identify the pitch of a sound the computer has to spot the fundamental frequency of that sound. Most sounds contain a whole stack of frequencies, that's what gives it it's tone. It's why instruments sound different and distinct from each other even when playing the same note. Amongst all these frequencies the fundamental denotes the actual perceived pitch. For the computer to accurately spot this is really very difficult. You can't just take the strongest frequency in a sound and call it pitch, well you can, but it takes an accurate player to generate notes where the computer can easily see what frequency is the strongest. I could go into frequency analysis is great depth but I won't because it's not very exciting.

There is 'pitch-to-MIDI' software available and some sequencers come with this built in. However, if you try to use it you will find that you will spend so much time editing the result afterwards that you may as well have put the notes in by hand, with your mouse.

It would be great if you could do it easily. That way you could sing into your sequencer and play it back like a whole orchestra, or use a flute rather than a MIDI keyboard. There are MIDI interfaces or converters available for some instruments, guitars are a good example and work really well. You can put a special pick-up on your guitar and a magic box will throw out surprisingly accurate MIDI information. Generally though, especially for the voice with its amazing combination of tones and harmonics, it's not very good.

*Glossary* **16**

**T**hese aren't absolute definitions, what do you think I am a professor? They are a explanation of a few of the terms I used, in the context of computer music.

**AES/EBU** Professional format for digital transfer using XLR or Cannon connectors. Stands for Audio Engineering Society/European Broadcasting Union.

**Analogue** In electronics this describes a continuously variable signal, something which is not restricted to exact values. In music this refers to the variable electronic signal of sound going through an electrical device. Sound waves are converted into a variable electrical signal by a magnetic device like a microphone which generates electricity in response to the varying pressure of sound waves. An analogue device is also described as being linear, and as having an output proportional to it's input. Hmmm tricky one to actually define but I hope by now that you have the general idea.

**Audio** Thought I'd been through this already have you still not got the hang of it? Okay, audio is sound waves in air, anything audible, anything you can hear. In our situation we like to call it music if we can. To be technical for a moment the average frequency range of human hearing is from 20Hz to 20kHz. You tend to lose it very quickly though, especially if you like listening to loud music.

**Audio Sequencer** A piece of software run on a computer which allows for the recording and arrangement of multiple audio tracks.

**CD quality** The quality or digital resolution at which audio CD's are recorded. 16 bit resolution, 44.1Khz sampling rate.

**Chorus** A modulation effect. Gives the impression of light vibrato or phasing, a kind of wobbly feel. Sounds nice!

**Compressor** Device used to restrict the dynamic range of a piece of audio.

**Decibel (dB)** This is basically a ratio and can be used to describe anything. It's often used in music to describe the difference in gain or attenuation of the amplitude of sound. Eg: boosting a signal by 6dB would mean that the signal has been boosted by a ratio of 2:1. It's a logarithmic scale and the ratio can be calculated using dB=20logx where x=ratio.

**Delay** An effect which creates a distinct echo.

**Digital** A representation of magnitude in whole numbers or digits. Computers are digital machines. In music, recording audio digitally means that the recording is represented on a digital device by the whole values of bits (digital audio).

**Dynamic range** The difference between the quietest and loudest sound.

**Enhancer** Device used to boost higher frequencies and harmonics to produce a brighter tone.

**Frequency** Cycles per second, measured in Hertz (Hz). How many times something happens per second.

**Full duplex** The ability of a soundcard or audio recording card installed in a computer to record and playback audio simultaneously.

**General Protection Fault** You'll see this from time to time and it means that your PC has crashed and it's time to restart your computer and hope that you remembered to save your work recently. There's no answer, no meaning, something to do with the computer trying to use the same bit of memory to do two things at once – duh! We love it really, makes life exciting.

**Hardware** The physical, touchable parts of a computer or other device.

**Hertz (Hz)** The unit of frequency which measures the number of cycles a waveform completes per second.

**Latency** The time delay between causing an event and that event actually occurring; e.g. the time between striking a key and hearing the sound of a software synth.

**MPEG** Motion Pictures Expert Group. A bunch of geezers who set up standards for multimedia.

**MIDI** Musical Instrument Digital Interface.

**MIDI device** Anything that responds to, or communicates with, MIDI information.

**MIDI module** A device which responds to MIDI information. Usually generates the sound of an instrument in response to a MIDI "note on" event.

**MIDI information** A stream of instructions created by a MIDI device.

**MIDI instrument** A term used to describe an individual program or patch within a MIDI device that refers to a sound.

**Monophonic** A single tone. Used to describe a synthesiser/MIDI instrument that can only produce a single note at a time.

**MTC** MIDI time code. The method by which MIDI tempo, position and start/stop can be linked to SMPTE.

**Polyphonic** A synthesiser/MIDI instrument that can produce more than a single tone at a time can be described as polyphonic.

**Polyphony** The number of tones, voices or notes a synthesiser/MIDI instrument can produce simultaneously.

**Quantisation** Moving MIDI notes (in terms of start time and length) to the nearest musical division. In other words it tidies up your sloppy timing. You can also quantise audio nowadays as well.

**Red Book** Specifications for the production of audio compact disks.

**Reverb** Short for reverberation, which is essentially 'echo'. When you hear an instrument being played you can also hear the echo of the instrument as the sound is reflected off walls and surfaces. Adding reverb to a recorded musical instrument gives the effect of space.

**Sample** Digital representation of audio.

**Sampling** The process of converting analogue audio into digital audio.

**Sampling rate** The number of times an analogue waveform is measured or sampled per second to convert it to digital.

**SCSI** Small Computer System Interface.

**SMPTE** Society of Motion Picture and Television Engineers. This is the most widely used form of synchronisation. It's a code which is recorded to tape (striped) and contains information on position and time frame. It enables two analogue tape machines to run in perfect time to one another. Originally used to sync film and music. For us it's most useful in that SMPTE can be converted to or from  MIDI Time code enabling us to sync MIDI sequencers and analogue tape machines together.

**Software** Written programs or procedures or rules and associated documentation pertaining to the operation of a computer system and that are stored in read/write memory. Okay, so its a program usually stuck onto your hard drive.

**Sound** See Audio.

**Synchronisation** The ability to link together two or more bits of gear so that they can share a common time reference.

**Synthesis** The artificial generation of a sound by electronic means.

**Synthesiser** A device which can synthesise sound by electronics.

**WAV** Or wave file. The digital audio file format used by Windows.

# Products

There is loads of stuff available for turning your computer into a music making machine. The following list is merely a selection of some of the more popular pieces of software and hardware currently available and is by no means definitive. If I've missed anything important out then I apologise but if I haven't seen it then they can't be doing a very good job of telling people about it!

For more in depth information on these products and others then point your browser to my companion web page which has links to manufacturers and other goodies: http://www.pc-music.com

## Software

### MIDI sequencers

Well, there's not much about anymore which is a pure MIDI sequencer. All the products which once were now contain at least some element of audio recording as well. No, I can't think of any.

### MIDI Sequencers/hard disk recording

I'll start with the three main players.

#### Emagic – Logic Audio
There's a range of four products from Emagic, each at a different level of sophistication.

*Micrologic AV*
Simple sequencer with up to 16 tracks of audio recording, 2 effect busses and 3 band equaliser. Also synchronises to Quicktime/AVI movies. Aimed at the beginner. RRP £99.

*Logic Audio Silver*
MIDI sequencing and 24 tracks of audio, 4 effects busses and 3 band EQ. Sample and MIDI controller editing. For the hobbyist and ambitious songwriter. RRP £199.

*Logic Audio Gold*
Full MIDI sequencing with scoring and 48 tracks of audio. 8 effect busses and 8 inserts. DirectX compatible for plug-ins. Advanced audio editing. Aimed at project studios and professionals. RRP £399.

*Logic Audio Platinum*
As Gold but with up to 96 tracks of audio and support for high end professional studio hardware. For professionals using the highest quality hardware. RRP £549.

**Steinberg – Cubase**
Four products in a similar vein as Emagic.

*Cubasis AV*
Simple sequencing an 8 tracks of audio. Quicktime/AVI synchronisation. RRP £129.

*Cubase VST (Virtual Studio Technology)*
Industry standard sequencing and 32 tracks of hard disk recording. Realtime effects processing with DirectX compatibility. Aimed at the project studio and professional. RRP £329.

*Cubase VST Score*
Same as above but with desk top publishing score abilities. RRP £499.

*Cubase VST/24*
Same as score but with added extensions for high end professional studio hardware and supports 24bit audio. RRP £649.

**Twelve Tone – Cakewalk**
This is one of the few programs that can run under Windows NT. It's always been on the PC platform so the program is very stable and is the industry standard in the USA, apparently.

*Home Studio*
Easy to use, simple sequencer and 4 track audio recording. RRP £99

*Professional Version 7*
This offers full sequencing and 8 track audio recording with realtime effects processing and DirectX. RRP £199.

*Pro Audio 8*
Complete sequencing and audio recording with clever virtual mixers of popular hardware. Easy to use and powerful. RRP £299.

### Other bits of good budget software

*Digital Orchestra Pro*
By Voyetra the company who owns Turtle Beach soundcards. Simple sequencing and hard disk recording. Really easy to use and surprisingly good. RRP £149.

*Evolution Studio Gold*
By Evolution. A remarkably cheap and easy sequencer and audio recorder. Some effects built in and also automatic accompaniment. RRP £149.

## Wave/sample editing

### Sound Forge (Sonic Foundry)
Stereo wave editing for the professional. Full of tools and editing functions, realtime effects processing and DirectX. Supports sample editing direct from hardware samplers via SCSI. RRP £349.

### Wavelab (Steinberg)
Stereo wave editing with the bias towards music mastering. Realtime effects and DirectX. Can master to CD from within the program. RRP £329.

## Notation software

Only two serious ones but there are a few others and budget ones.

### Finale (Coda)
Full orchestral scoring. A publishing tool for manuscript printing, contains everything you need to write and print scores. RRP £499.

### Sibelius
Very fast and creative score writing software. Used by professional composers and music schools. RRP £695.

## Plug-ins

These are arriving all the time from all sorts of different places. Some of the main players are:

### Waves

*Native Power Pack*
Contains a great reverb, compressor, stereo imaging and loads of EQ. RRP £399.

*EZ Waves*
A budget package with a reverb, compressor and EQ. RRP £129.

## Opcode

*Fusion*
Effects with the slightly unusual Vinyl, Vocode and Filter. RRP £around 100 each.

### Steinberg
Lot's of different ones available from de-noises to filters, the Red Valve-it and TC Works Native range. RRP from £99.

## Soft synths

Here's a few software based synths and samplers that I have come into contact with. More and more appear daily so check my web page for a more up to date list (www.pc-music.com).

### Native Instruments

*Generator*
Intense and powerful modular analogue synth. RRP £169.

*Transformator*
Intense and powerful modular sampler. RRP £169.

*Reaktor*
Combines Generator and Transformator in an intense and powerful package. RRP £249.

*Dynamo*
DirectX effect plug-in creator based upon Generator. RRP £99.

### Koblo

*Vibra6000*
Monophonic software synth, great for basslines. RRP £69.

*Vibra9000*
Advanced monophonic soft synth, green and funky. RRP £99.

*Gamma9000*
Multi-timbral sample based drum synth, purple and funky. RRP
£99.

*Stella9000*
Advanced polyphonic sampler, blue and funky. RRP £149.

**Bitheadz**

*Retro AS1*
Multi-timbral analogue synth. 1000's of presets. RRP £129.

*Unity DS1*
Comprehensive sampler synth, accepts many formats. RRP £249.

*Osmosis*
The sample conversion facilities of Unity, Akai-Wave etc. RRP £69.

**GigaSampler (Nemesys)**
First effective soft sampler. 16 part, 64 note polyphony, up to 2GB
sample space. RRP £549, LE version available RRP £149 loses
editing software, Akai support, 1GB piano sample and audio
capture facility.

**Rebirth RB338 (Steinberg)**
Faithful model of MC303 (x2) TR808 and TR909. RRP £149.

# Hardware

## Soundcards

There's only a couple of all-in-one soundcards that I recommend,
there are plenty more but most are designed for games not music.

**Turtle Beach**
A name synonymous with music soundcards, been making them for
ages. They have a whole range but here are the best two:

*Pinnacle*
20bit converters, stereo audio in/out, Kurzweil GM synth engine,
joystick port MIDI interface. Option for adding RAM for sample
playback. Upgradable with a daughter board synth. RRP £299.

*Fiji*
As above but without synth or sample option. RRP £199. Both can
have a digital option fitted giving SP/DIF in and out.

### Terratec

*EWS64L*
Constantly changing options with this card but offers lots of features including sample playback, on board synth, two MIDI ports. Has an option for a drive bay unit giving easy access to the ins and outs and adds SPDIF digital in and out and optical out. Also they have a Waldorf Microwave option which puts a powerful synth in the drive bay. RRP £329.

## MIDI Interfaces

Not a very exciting area but there are three companies who produce good hardware MIDI interfaces, Midiman, Opcode and MOTU. Simple 1in 1out interfaces start at around fifty quid all the way up to about 600 for 8in 8out with synchronisation.

## Audio cards

This is where the market has exploded recently giving incredible power and quality to the PC music making experience. Some of these could also be called 'Soundcards' but the term doesn't do them justice.

### DMAN 2044 (Midiman)
20bit 4 in 4 out PCI card. Two cards can be used together for 8 in and out. RRP £249.

### Darla (Event)
20bit 2 in 8 out PCI card. RRP £299.

### Gina (Event)
As above but with SPDIF in and out and a breakout box. RRP £399.

### Layla (Event)
20bit 8 in 10 out with SPDIF and MIDI in/out/thru on a rack mount breakout box. RRP £899.

### Audiowerk8 (Emagic)
18bit 2in 8out with SP/DIF in/out PCI card designed for Logic Audio. Breakout box available. RRP £399.

### Wave/8.24 (Gadget Labs)
24 bit hardware interface giving 8 analogue in/out via a 19 inch rack attatched to a  PCI card. RRP £449.

### Korg 1212PCI
PCI card with 12 ins and outs. 8 on ADAT optical, 2 on SP/DIF and 2 analogue. RRP £599.

**Audiomedia III (Digidesign)**
The original hard disk recording PCI card. Stereo in/out and SPDIF. RRP £399.

**Audio Production Studio (E-MU Systems)**
PCI card with drive bay interface which features 64 voice
Studio sampling, hard disk recording and DSP effects. Professional inputs and outputs and comes with stacks of software. RRP £449.

**DSP Factory (Yamaha)**
PCI hard disk recording card with 24 track digital mixing and professional quality effects. Two drive bay expansions can be added to give 8X8 professional in/outs. RRP £599.

**SW1000XG (Yamaha)**
PCI hard disk recording card with an on board professional quality synth modelled on the MU100R. RRP £449.

**MOTU 2408 (Mark of the Unicorn)**
Hardware interface giving 24 in/out: 8 analogue, 8 ADAT optical and 8 TDIF optical. Top quality converters. RRP £995.

**Project II (Digidesign)**
At last, an affordable solution from the Pro Tools people. PCI 8 track hard disk recording interface card. RRP £799, requires an external convertor like the 882 interface.

**Mixtreme (Soundscape)**
Just to be different this card uses twin Tascam TDIF optical to run 16 tracks in and out of a PC. Stable option from the best PC based hard disk recorder manufacturers. RRP £499.

**Pulsar (Creamware)**
Fully integrated DSP and routing card combining audio recording, mixing, effects, soft synthesis and sampling. Twin ADAT, SP/DIF and analogue I/O. RRP £999.

## Professional systems

Although the lines between what is deemed 'professional' are increasingly blurred there are a number of products which are aimed at the no nonsense people who demand a fully working system with the minimum of fuss, and money is less of an issue. It has to be said that these systems do rock, although many of the bits of software and hardware mentioned earlier can be brought up to this standard.

### PARIS (Ensoniq)

Pro Audio Recording Integrated System. This is a combined system of software and hardware delivering up to 128 tracks of audio recording. The system includes a hardware interface plugged into the PC via a PCI card. The interface is completely modular allowing you to expand your system as necessary, add another 8 inputs, or an ADAT interface.

The software is very pretty and has a great graphical feel and allows all the usual editing and mixing. The nicest part of this system is integrated hardware mixer. This allows for real tactile control over 16 tracks, level, EQ, transport controls, it's just so much easier than using a mouse. RRP £2500 for the basic system with 4in and 4out.

### Samplitude 2496 (SEK'D)

A bold step into the new professional digital format of 24bit/96kHz. Using an advanced version of Samplitude Pro software combined with some of the best A/D D/A converters available connected via their Prodif 96 PCI card.

The software includes tonnes of effects and dynamic processing and has a facility to burn mixes direct to CD. It can handle up to 999 stereo tracks and can apply effects and mixing to sources being routed through without recording them. The sound quality is stunning but tends to eat hard drives for breakfast. RRP £2400.

### Lexicon Studio System (Lexicon)

This is a hardware solution that will run with other people's software like Cubase VST. The hardware consists of a PCI card, more can be added, that provides the interface for a powerful rack mount converter. The converter gives stereo balanced in and out and ADAT optical. The system removes all the processing load from the PC and makes Cubase run very efficiently.

The best part of this system is the daughter board version of Lexicon's PCM90 reverb module which retails for a couple of grand. It provides outstanding reverb plug-ins from within Cubase. RRP £2695.

### Soundscape SSHDR1 (Soundscape)

This is the one that the rest (excluding Pro Tools) are trying to live up to. Been doing it for years on 386MHz PC's and still can! It consists of a 19 inch rack mount hardware unit with stereo in and 4 outputs and an internal hard drive. The editing software that comes with it is plain and functional giving 8 actual and 64 virtual tracks. The PC acts simply as the control centre and is rarely called upon to any actual work. Very simple, very solid, very workable.

Multiple units can be strung together to give more in/outs and more tracks, removable hard drives can be added, DSP plug-ins can be utilised. Runs seamlessly with video and its synchronisation is perfect. Doesn't sound very exciting really but this system will not crash or fall over or run out of processing power. It works all the time and is easy to use. RRP from around £3000 up to as much as you like.

## Pro Tools 24 (Digidesign)

A continually expanding system of hardware and software although it's the hardware that makes this system special. Rock solid audio recording, editing and synchronisation. They have special DSP 'Farms' which take all the processing load so running plug-in effects (a concept Digidesign invented) is no problem, use as many as you like. No latency, no delays, no crashes, no glitches, just solid performance. There are also hardware control surfaces (like mixers) that can be attached to take the work off the mouse. This was always the best reason to buy an Apple Mac, but you can now keep it real with Windows NT. RRP project studios from about £3000, professional setups around £10,000.

There are others, some of them running into many many thousands of pounds, but I feel that they perhaps go beyond the scope of this book.

# 18 General MIDI

## General MIDI instrument list

| No. | Name | No. | Name |
|-----|------|-----|------|
| 1 | Acoustic grand piano | 21 | Reed organ |
| 2 | Bright acoustic grand piano | 22 | Accordion (Francias) |
| 3 | Electric grand piano | 23 | Harmonica |
| 4 | Honky-tonk piano | 24 | Bandoneon |
| 5 | Electric piano 1 | 25 | Nylon string guitar |
| 6 | Electric piano 2 | 26 | Steel string guitar |
| 7 | Harpsichord | 27 | Jazz guitar |
| 8 | Clav | 28 | Clean guitar |
| 9 | Celeste | 29 | Muted/damped guitar |
| 10 | Glockenspiel | 30 | Overdrive guitar |
| 11 | Music box | 31 | Distortion guitar |
| 12 | Vibraphone | 32 | Guitar harmonics |
| 13 | Marimba | 33 | Acoustic/wood bass |
| 14 | Xylophone | 34 | Fingered electric bass |
| 15 | Tubular bells | 35 | Picked electric bass |
| 16 | Santur | 36 | Fretless bass |
| 17 | Full organ | 37 | Slap bass 1 |
| 18 | Percussive organ | 38 | Slap bass 2 |
| 19 | Rock organ | 39 | Synth bass 1 |
| 20 | Church organ | 40 | Synth bass 2 |

| No. | Name | No. | Name |
|---|---|---|---|
| 41 | Violin | 85 | Charang (lead 5) |
| 42 | Viola | 86 | Solo vox (lead 6) |
| 43 | Cello | 87 | Fifth saw wave (lead 7) |
| 44 | Contrabass | 88 | Bass and lead (lead 8) |
| 45 | Tremolo strings | 89 | Fantasia (pad 1) |
| 46 | Pizzicato strings | 90 | Warm pad (pad 2) |
| 47 | Harp | 91 | Polysynth (pad 3) |
| 48 | Timpani | 92 | Space voice (pad 4) |
| 49 | Ensemble strings | 93 | Bowed glass (pad 5) |
| 50 | Slow attack strings | 94 | Metal pad (pad 6) |
| 51 | Synth strings 1 | 95 | Halo pad (pad 7) |
| 52 | Synth strings 2 | 96 | Sweep pad (pad 8) |
| 53 | Choir – aahs | 97 | Ice rain (FX 1) |
| 54 | Choir – oohs | 98 | Soundtrack (FX 2) |
| 55 | Synth vox | 99 | Crystal (FX 3) |
| 56 | Orchestra hit | 100 | Atmosphere (FX 4) |
| 57 | Trumpet | 101 | Brightness (FX 5) |
| 58 | Trombone | 102 | Goblin (FX 6) |
| 59 | Tuba | 103 | Echo drops (FX 7) |
| 60 | Muted trumpet | 104 | Star theme (FX 8) |
| 61 | French horn | 105 | Sitar |
| 62 | Brass | 106 | Banjo |
| 63 | Synth brass 1 | 107 | Shamisen |
| 64 | Synth brass 2 | 108 | Koto |
| 65 | Soprano sax | 109 | Kalimba |
| 66 | Alto sax | 110 | Bagpipes |
| 67 | Tenor sax | 111 | Fiddle |
| 68 | Baritone sax | 112 | Shanai |
| 69 | Oboe | 113 | Tinkle bell |
| 70 | English horn | 114 | Agogo |
| 71 | Bassoon | 115 | Steel drums |
| 72 | Clarinet | 116 | Woodblock |
| 73 | Piccolo | 117 | Taiko |
| 74 | Flute | 118 | Melodic tom tom |
| 75 | Recorder | 119 | Synth drum |
| 76 | Pan flute | 120 | Reverse cymbal |
| 77 | Bottle blow | 121 | Guitar fret noise |
| 78 | Shakuhachi | 122 | Breath noise |
| 79 | Whistle | 123 | Seashore |
| 80 | Ocarina | 124 | Bird |
| 81 | Square wave (lead 1) | 125 | Telephone |
| 82 | Saw wave (lead 2) | 126 | Helicopter |
| 83 | Synth calliope (lead 3) | 127 | Applause |
| 84 | Chiffer lead (lead 4) | 128 | Gunshot |

## General MIDI drum map

| Key | Note | Instrument | Key | Note | Instrument |
|---|---|---|---|---|---|
| 35 | B | Acoustic kick drum | 59 | B | Ride cymbal 2 |
| 36 | C | Electric kick drum | 60 | C | Hi bongo |
| 37 | C# | Side stick/stick across | 61 | C# | Low bongo |
| 38 | D | Acoustic snare drum | 62 | D | Mute hi conga |
| 39 | D# | Hand clap | 63 | D# | Open hi conga |
| 40 | E | Electric snare drum | 64 | E | Low conga |
| 41 | F | Low floor tom | 65 | F | High timbale |
| 42 | F# | Closed hi-hat | 66 | F# | Low timbale |
| 43 | G1 | High floor tom | 67 | G | High agogo |
| 44 | G# | Pedal hi-hat | 68 | G# | Low agogo |
| 45 | A | Low tom | 69 | A | Cabasa |
| 46 | A# | Open hi-hat | 70 | A# | Maracas |
| 47 | B | Low mid tom | 71 | B | Short whistle |
| 48 | C | High mid tom | 72 | C | Long whistle |
| 49 | C# | Crash cymbal 1 | 73 | C# | Short guiro |
| 50 | D | High tom | 74 | D | Long guiro |
| 51 | D# | Ride cymbal 1 | 75 | D# | Claves |
| 52 | E | China cymbal | 76 | E | High wood block |
| 53 | F | Ride bell | 77 | F | Low wood block |
| 54 | F# | Tambourine | 78 | F# | Mute cuica |
| 55 | G | Splash cymbal | 79 | G | Open cuica |
| 56 | G# | Cowbell | 80 | G# | Muted triangle |
| 57 | A | Crash cymbal 2 | 81 | A | Open triangle |
| 58 | A# | Vibraslap | | | |

## General MIDI control change table

| Control No | Name | Control No | Name |
|---|---|---|---|
| 0 | Bank select | 75 | Undefined/reverb |
| 1 | Modulation wheel | 76 | Undefined/delay |
| 2 | Breath controller | 77 | Undefined/pitch transposer |
| 3 | Undefined | | |
| 4 | Foot controller | 78 | Undefined/flange or chor. |
| 5 | Portamento time | | |
| 6 | Data entry | 79 | Undefined/special effects |
| 7 | Main volume | | |
| 8 | Balance | 80–83 | General purpose 5-8 |
| 9 | Undefined | 84 | Portamento control |
| 10 | Pan | 85–90 | Undefined |
| 11 | Expression | 91 | Effects depth (effect 1) |
| 12 | Effect control 1 | 92 | Tremolo depth (effect 2) |
| 13 | Effect control 2 | 93 | Chorus depth (effect 3) |
| 14–15 | Undefined | 94 | Celeste depth (effect 4) |
| 16–19 | General purpose 1–4 | 95 | Phaser depth (effect 5) |
| 20–31 | Undefined | 96 | Data increment |
| 32–63 | LSB for ctrl changes 0–31 | 97 | Data decrement |
| | | 98 | Non-reg param. no. LSB |
| 64 | Damper/sustain pedal | 99 | Non-reg param. no. MSB |
| 65 | Portamento | 100 | Reg parameter no. LSB |
| 66 | Sostenuto | 101 | Reg parameter no. MSB |
| 67 | Soft pedal | 102/119 | Undefined |
| 68 | Legato footswitch | 120 | All sound off |
| 69 | Hold 2 | 121 | Reset all controllers |
| 70 | Sound variation/exciter | 122 | Local control |
| 71 | Harm content/comp | 123 | All notes off |
| 72 | Release time/distortion | 124 | Omni mode off |
| 73 | Attack time/equaliser | 125 | Omni mode on |
| 74 | Brightness/expander or noise gate | 126 | Mono mode on |
| | | 127 | Poly mode on |

# Contacts

he listed phone numbers refer to the distributors in the UK although the products are available all over the world.

Bitheadz (Turnkey) 0171 3795148
Retro AS-1, Unity DS-1, Osmosis
http://www.bitheadz.com

Coda (Etc) 01706 219999
Finale
http://www.codamusic.com

Emagic (Sound Technology) 01462 480500
Logic Audio, Audiowerk8.
http://www.emagic.de

E-MU Systems Inc. 0131 6536556
Audio Production Studio
http://www.emu.com

Ensoniq (E-MU) 0131 6536556
PARIS
http://www.ensoniq.com

Event (Key Audio) 01245 344001
Darla, Gina, Layla
http://www.event1.com

Digidesign 01753 653322
Pro Tools
http://www.digidesign.com

Koblo (Turnkey) 0171 3795148
Vibra9000, Gamma9000, Stella9000
http://www.koblo.com

Korg 01908 857130
1212PCI card
http://www.korg.com

Midiman 01309 671301
Audio cards, MIDI interfaces
http://www.midiman.net

MOTU (Musictrack) 01462 812010
MIDI interfaces, 2408 audio interface
http://www.motu.com

Native Instruments (Turnkey) 0171 3795148
Generator, Transformator, Reaktor, Dynamo
http://native-instruments.com

Nemesys Music Technology (Turnkey) 0171 379 5148
Gigasampler
http://www.nemesysmusic.com

Opcode (SCV) 0171 9231892
Midi interfaces, Studio Vision audio sequencing, Fusion Plug-in effects
http://www.scvlondon.co.uk

Voyetra (Arbiter) 0181 2075050
Digital Orchestrator
http://www.voyetra.com

SEK'D (SCV) 0171 9231892
Samplitude 2496, audio interface cards
http://www.sekd.com

Sibelius 0800 4583111
Sibelius notation software
http://www.sibelius.com

Sonic Foundry (SCV) 0171 9231892
Sound Forge, Acid
http://www.sonicfoundry.com

Soundscape 01222 450120
SSHDR1, Mixtreme
http://www.soundscape-digital.com/

Steinberg (Arbiter) 0181 20275050
Cubase VST, Wavelab, Rebirth, Recycle, BBox, Plug-in effects
http://www.steinberg-us.com

Turtle Beach (Etc) 01706 219999
Soundcards
http://www.tbeach.com

Twelve Tone (Etc) 01706 219999
Cakewalk
http://www.cakewalk.com

Waves (SCV) 0171 9231892
Plug-in effects
http://www.scvlondon.co.uk

Yamaha 01908 369254
DSP Factory, SW1000XG
http://www.yamaha.co.uk

Links to these manufacturers and others can be found on my web page designed as a companion to this book:

**http://www.pc-music.com**

So, where can I buy all this gear to make beautiful music on my PC? Well, a good place to start would be Turnkey in Charing Cross Road in London. They stock almost everything I've been talking about and you get the best advice there because it just happens to be where I work. So, drop in and ask for me and I'll do my best to sort you out with whatever you need.

Turnkey/Soho Soundhouse
114-116 Charing Cross Road
London
WC2H 0DT
0171 379 5148
0171 379 0093 (fax)
robinv@turnkey.demon.co.uk
http://www.turnkey.uk.com

# Index

ACID, 45, 79
ADAT, 70
ADC, 7, 70 ,73
AES, 95
analogue, 7, 95
analogue modular synthesis, 42
analogue synthesis, 16, 42
analogue synths, 78
analogue-to-digital converter, 7
Apple Mac, 84
Arrange window, 17, 26
audio, 5 – 7, 95
audio cards, 104
audio editing, 29
audio sequencer, 23, 95
audio track editing, 29

bank, 19
binary, 8
bit, 8
bit rate, 8
Bitheadz, 103

Cakewalk, 20, 30
CD quality, 9, 89, 96
CD-R, 91
CD-RW, 93
chorus, 96
compression, 50
compressor, 96
contacts, 112

control panel, 61
copyright, 51, 53
Creative Labs Sound Blaster, 9
Cubase, 100
Cubase VST, 17, 28
cut-off point, 78

DAC, 7, 73
dance music, 74
DAT, 10, 70, 72, 91
decibel, 96
delay, 96
Digidesign, 24
digital, 7, 96
digital ins, 10
digital mixer, 70, 72
digital mixing desk, 11
digital outs, 10
digital-to-analogue converter, 7
DirectX, 36
drum grid editor, 20
drum sound, 76
dynamic range, 96

EBU, 95
effects, 26, 28, 35, 73
EIDE, 92
Emagic Logic, 99
enhancer, 96
EQ, 26, 28, 33, 35
equalisation, 26

error correction, 9
event list editor, 21

filter, 77
Finale, 101
FM synth, 63
frequency, 96
full duplex, 96
FX, 26, 28, 33

General MIDI control change table, 111
General MIDI drum map, 110
General MIDI instrument list, 108
General MIDI, 14
general protection fault, 96
Generator, 44
GigaSampler, 44, 103
GS, 15
guitar, 80

hard disk digital audio recording, 3
hard disk recording, 23, 61, 99
hardware, 96
hertz, 8, 96
hit, 76

internet, 48

joystick, 64
joystick port, 5, 6, 12, 67

key edit, 19
Koblo, 102

latency, 96
Lexicon Studio System, 106
line in, 6
line out, 6
Liquid Audio, 53
Logic Audio, 21, 26, 27
loop, 76
low-pass filter, 77

matrix editor, 19
Media Player, 57
mic in, 6
MIDI, 2, 5, 11, 97
MIDI channel, 17
MIDI controller, 20. 21, 72
MIDI device, 2, 11, 97
MIDI event, 21
MIDI file, 14, 40, 49, 58
MIDI guitar, 82
MIDI IN, 12, 18, 67, 72
MIDI information, 97
MIDI instrument, 97

MIDI interface, 12, 14, 18, 65, 67, 69, 104
MIDI module, 97
MIDI OUT, 12, 18, 67, 72
MIDI port, 12
MIDI sequencer, 2, 99
MIDI sequencing, 16
MIDI synthesiser, 67
MIDI THRU, 12
MIDI time code, 97
MIDI tracks, 17
MIDI window, 63
mix down, 70
mixer, 27, 69
modular synthesis, 42
modules, 42
monophonic, 97
MP3, 51
MPEG, 97
MPU-401, 12, 63
MTC, 97
multimedia, 62
multitimbrality, 2
multitrack, 23, 67

native instruments, 102
non-destructive editing, 29
normalisation, 30
notation, 4, 22, 38
notation software, 101
note off, 2
note on, 2, 12

orchestral scoring, 38

PARIS, 106
patch, 11 19
patch change, 2
PC, 84
piano roll editor, 19
pitch bend, 12
pitch shift, 31
plug-in, 35, 73, 101
polyphonic, 97
polyphony, 9, 97
Pro Tools 24, 25, 107
program, 11, 19
program change, 12

quantisation, 97
Quicktime, 52

RAM, 7
re-writable CDs, 93
real-time, 28
RealAudio, 51
Rebirth, 43, 103

recording controls, 60
recycle, 76
Red Book Standard, 92
Red Book, 97
resolution, 8
resonant filter, 78
reverb, 97
Roland, 15, 41

sample, 97
sample digital audio editing, 3
sample editing, 33, 101
sampler, 7, 75
sampling, 7, 97
sampling rate, 8, 97
Samplitude, 106
scanning, 40
score editors, 22
score writing, 38
SCSI, 92, 97
SCSI AV drive, 88
SCSI hard drives, 70
sequencer, 12, 16
Sibelius, 39, 101
signal-to-noise ratio, 10
SMPTE, 97
soft synths, 102
software, 98
software sampler, 8, 76
software sampling, 44
software synthesis, 41
Sound Forge, 34, 101
sound modules, 11
Sound Recorder, 60
soundcard, 5, 7, 57, 62, 67, 103
Soundscape SSHDR1, 106
Soundscape, 24
speaker out, 6

Steinberg, 102
Steinberg Cubase, 100
streaming audio, 51
studio, 66
synchronisation, 98
synthesis, 98
synthesiser, 11, 98
system, 65

tabulature, 40
time stretching, 31
tone generators, 11
trigger, 7, 8
Turtle Beach, 103
Twelve Tone - Cakewalk, 100

velocity, 2, 20
Virtual acoustic modelling, 45
VL, 45
volume control, 59

WAV, 98
wave digital audio editing, 3
wave editing, 33, 101
wave files, 3
Wavelab, 34, 101
Waves, 102
wavetable, 11, 63
Windows 95/98, 57
Windows NT, 85
Windows, 57
World Wide Web, 48
WWW, 48

XG, 15

Yamaha, 15, 41, 45

# Fast Guide to Cubase VST

## Simon Millward

352 pp • 244 x 172 mm • ISBN 1870775 57 0

£21.95 inc P&P

★ For PC and Mac versions
★ Installation and setting up
★ MIDI and audio features of Cubase VST
★ Hands on projects
★ Steinberg and third party plug-ins
★ Time saving short cuts

*The Fast Guide to Cubase* VST provides the essential information for quickly getting into Steinberg's Cubase VST MIDI sequencing and audio recording package. The book covers all the important aspects of the program including audio and MIDI recording and 'virtual studio technology'.

Installation and setting up of the program are explained, and detailed information on how to record, edit, process and mix digital audio and how to use EQ and effects are all featured. A number of Steinberg and third party plug-in's are explored, and the book shows how to get the best from processing techniques such as compression, gating and limiting. The software is also tested with a range of PC audio cards.

Projects and tutorials throughout the book describe Cubase VST in a number of recording and processing roles, providing valuable insights into how best to use the program for specific tasks.

*The Fast Guide to Cubase* VST is the ideal companion for all users of the software, from the home sound recordist / musician to the audio professional.

**Press reviews**

'Projects and tutorials describe valuable insights into how best to use Cubase VST for specific tasks, with plenty of time saving shortcuts' *Sound on Sound* – Nov 1998
'Great ... background information and walkthrough tutorial features on almost every feature ... a lot more help than the manual and sheds light on bits of Cubase you never knew existed' *Future Music* – Jan 1999
'A real knowledge base for any user ... the audio side is excellent ... well worth the investment' *Basique – Club Cubase magazine*

# PC Publishing

Export House, 130 Vale Road, Tonbridge, Kent TN9 1SP, UK
Tel 01732 770893 • Fax 01732 770268 • e-mail info@pc-publishing.co.uk
Website http://www.pc-publishing.co.uk

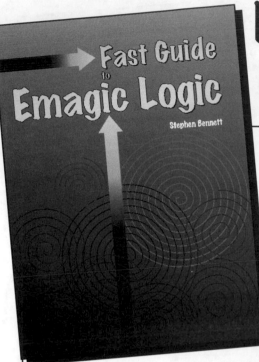

# Fast Guide to Emagic Logic

**£16.95 inc P&P**

## Stephen Bennett

240 pp • 244 x 172 mm
ISBN 1870775 55 4

★ For Atari, Macintosh and PC
★ Setting up the program
★ Achieve more musical results
★ User tips and tricks
★ Answers to commonly asked questions
★ Reference for most used functions

Making music is the raison d'etre of Emagic Logic, and this book helps you do just that. Logic is a completely flexible, totally user programmable, object orientated program and can be set up in many ways. This has led to its 'difficult' reputation, and It can appear daunting to the beginner, as well as to the more experienced user migrating from a more traditional sequencing package.

This book takes both types of user from the setting up of the program on Atari, Macintosh and PC platforms, right through to using Logic to make music.

This book describes Logic set-ups that will be useful to a typical user, while introducing some of Logic's more esoteric functions. It also serves as a handy reference to some of Logic's most used functions and contains some tips and tricks to help you with your music making.

Contents: Getting started with Logic, Using Logic, The Score editor, The Environment, The Arrange page, The Event list editor, The Matrix editor, The Transport bar, The Hyper editor, Key commands, Other useful Logic information, Logic menus, Preferences and song settings, Glossary, Logic and the Internet, Index

## PC Publishing

Export House, 130 Vale Road, Tonbridge, Kent TN9 1SP, UK
Tel 01732 770893 • Fax 01732 770268 • e-mail info@pc-publishing.co.uk
Website http://www.pc-publishing.co.uk

# Making music with digital audio

Direct to disk recording on the PC

## Ian Waugh

£16.95 inc P&P

244 x 172 mm * 256 pp
ISBN 1870775 51 1

☆ How to assess your requirements
☆ How to cut through the tech spec jargon
☆ What hardware you 'really' need
☆ How to back up your digital data
☆ How to troubleshoot effectively

The future is digital. Computers have revolutionised the recording and music-making business. Digital audio gives you more flexibility, higher quality and more creative power than multi-track tape recorders. This leading-edge technology is available now to all PC users – and it need not cost the earth.

In this practical and clearly-written book, Ian Waugh explains all aspects of the subject from digital audio basics to putting together a system to suit your own music requirements.

Using the minimum of technical language, the book explains exactly what you need to know about:

☆ Sound and digital audio
☆ Basic digital recording principles
☆ Sample rates and resolutions
☆ Consumer sound cards and dedicated digital audio cards

On a practical level you will learn about, sample editing, digital multi-tracking, digital FX processing, integrating MIDI and digital audio, using sample CDs, mastering to DAT and direct to CD, digital audio and Multimedia

This book is for every musician who wants to be a part of the most important development in music since the invention of the gramophone. It's affordable, it's flexible, it's powerful and it's here now! It's digital and it's the future of music making.

## PC Publishing

Export House, 130 Vale Road, Tonbridge, Kent TN9 1SP, UK
Tel 01732 770893 • Fax 01732 770268 • e-mail info@pc-publishing.co.uk
Website http://www.pc-publishing.co.uk

# Music on the Internet

**Ian Waugh**

256 pp • 244 x 172 mm • ISBN 1870775 58 9

The Internet is the largest music store, encyclopedia and software library in the world. In fact, it is the world! For musicians it's a treasure trove packed with information, news, software, sounds and music files. Through it you can contact the most knowledgeable people in the music business ... if you know where to look. In this practical, easy-to-read and information-packed book, Ian Waugh shows musicians exactly where to look and demonstrates how they can use the Internet to:

★ Get free music software and commercial demos
★ Get updates for their existing software
★ Find out about new products weeks before details appear in the press
★ Get help from manufacturers, developers and fellow musicians

In clear, jargon-free terms it explains:

★ All about the World Wide Web
★ About Web browsers
★ All about Web addresses – URLs
★ How to use Newsgroups and Mailing lists
★ How to Power Search the Web like a pro
★ The importance of high speed Net connections
★ Which modem you really need
★ How to download software

The book also contains the Web addresses of over 700 sites so you can find  what you want quickly and without delay. These include music information,  on-line magazines, music hardware manufacturers, music software  developers, shareware, sound files, music retailers, music publishers,  record companies, copyright information, music organisations, sites about  composition, artists and user groups.

If you're already on-line, this book will show you how to make the most of your Internet access. If you're not on-line – it will show why you ought to be!

£17.95 inc P&P

## PC Publishing

Export House, 130 Vale Road, Tonbridge, Kent TN9 1SP, UK
Tel 01732 770893 • Fax 01732 770268 • e-mail info@pc-publishing.co.uk
Website http://www.pc-publishing.co.uk